T0149758

Democracy Under Siege

Don't Let Them Lock It Down!

Democracy Under Siege

Don't Let Them Lock It Down!

Frank Furedi

Winchester, UK
Washington, USA

JOHN HUNT PUBLISHING

First published by Zero Books, 2021
Zero Books is an imprint of John Hunt Publishing Ltd., No. 3 East St., Alresford,
Hampshire SO24 9EE, UK
office@jhpbooks.com
www.johnhuntpublishing.com
www.zero-books.net

For distributor details and how to order please visit the 'Ordering' section on our website.

Text copyright: Frank Furedi 2020

ISBN: 978 1 78904 628 1
978 1 78904 629-8 (ebook)
Library of Congress Control Number: 2020943298

A CIP catalogue record for this book is available from the British Library.

Design: Stuart Davies

UK: Printed and bound by CPI Group (UK) Ltd, Croydon, CR0 4YY
Printed in North America by CPI GPS partners

We operate a distinctive and ethical publishing philosophy in
all areas of our business, from our global network of authors to
production and worldwide distribution.

Contents

Foreword: Democracy Panic

The idea for this book first began to take shape one night in June 2018 in Amsterdam after a talk I gave at the De Ballie cultural centre[1]. I was invited to explain why I believed that the rise of populism in Europe reflected a step forward for democracy. Throughout the evening members of a mainly anti-populist audience challenged my views; many of them insisted that 'democracy had gone too far'. When I replied that you can rarely have 'too much democracy', a member of the audience stood up and with a look of incredulity asked, 'Professor Furedi do you actually believe that democracy is good in and of itself'? He looked even more shocked when I replied 'yes'. Like many Western intellectuals, he possessed a narrow, instrumentalist view of democracy and took the view that it was OK, when it brought about the right results.

Since that night in Amsterdam I have frequently encountered the claim that democracy is a means to an end rather than an important value in and of itself. The prevalence of such sentiments is not surprising since in the current era, the normative foundation for democracy is shallow and, as I argue, there is little cultural valuation for this outlook. Scaremongering about the threat of 'too much democracy' is widespread and those who wish democracy further are condemned as populists. Since June 2016, when the British electorate voted for Brexit, opponents of this decision often resort to a language of panic when they discuss democracy.

Democracy Panic regards populism as a disease that can infect the body politic. 'I think what we have at the moment is a populist virus,' complains former UK Prime Minister Tony Blair's spin doctor, Alastair Campbell[2]. According to a professor of politics, populism is a 'recurrent autoimmune disease of democracy'[3]. During the coronavirus epidemic, some

1

speculated that this was a 'virus that could kill populism or make it stronger'[4]. With a hint of hope, one *Wall Street Journal* commentator asked, 'Will coronavirus kill populism?'[5]. Indeed, populism is sometimes characterised as a pathology not unlike Covid-19 and frequently it invites the diagnosis of 'too much democracy'. 'Too Much Democracy Is Bad For Democracy' warns a headline in *The Atlantic*[6]. *The Economist* concurs and warns that 'too much democracy threatens freedom'[7].

Historically, opponents of democracy were unambiguously open about their hostility towards both democracy and the people, the *demos*. They regarded democracy as a virus – not unlike Covid-19 – capable of dangerous contagion. In the 1840s, the hard-line former British foreign secretary the Viscount of Castlereagh described 'democratic contagion' as a 'pernicious force' spreading through the 'chief parts of the civilized earth'[8]. In the twenty-first century, it is widely recognised that governments require a degree of public consent and therefore cannot openly describe democracy as a 'pernicious force'. Instead it is through the narrative of *anti-populism* that such sentiments tend to be indirectly expressed.

Outwardly, anti-populism presents itself as a response to the threat of fascism, xenophobia and the politics of hate. Anti-populism relies on a rhetoric that portrays those it calls populists as a danger to a democratic and tolerant way of life. The anti-populist script frequently resorts to drawing facile comparisons between Nazi Germany and the behaviour of twenty-first century populist movements. Such misguided comparisons frequently indict democracy itself. They claim that it was democracy that brought Hitler to power[9]. Yet anyone with a knowledge of history knows that the Nazis had to physically destroy democracy – kill and arrest thousands of their opponents – before they staged a coup that allowed Hitler to rise to power. It was not through democracy but through the violent destruction of democratic practices – freedom of expression, freedom of assembly and the right to vote of those detained and arrested – that the Nazis gained power.

The unfortunate tendency to accuse populist opponents of being 'just like Hitler' not only distorts history but also trivialises the most tragic event of the modern era. The usage of this defamation, as a health warning about 'too much democracy', is symptomatic of a profound sense of mistrust and often of hostility towards people who vote the wrong way. The emergence of *Democracy Panic*, the fear of rejection by the people, is one of the most disturbing developments within Western elite politics. Outwardly, Democracy Panic appears as an expression of genuine concern about the future of democracy but on close inspection it becomes evident that its anxiety is focused on 'too much democracy'.

In recent times, disdain for democracy and for the moral and intellectual capacity of the electorate has acquired a powerful influence over public life. Alarmist claims about the threat of too much democracy inevitably draw on the ideas of the originators of this idea, the anti-democratic philosophers of ancient Greece. Commentaries praising the anti-democratic warnings of Plato and other ancient philosophers are frequently hurled at the threat of the virus of democracy[10]. In this book, I take a radically opposite view. This study aims to counter the different forms assumed by animosity towards democracy through the ages, with a positive affirmation of the principle and the value of democracy. It seeks to provide readers with an understanding of why democracy can never be taken for granted and why, yet again in the twenty-first century, it needs to be defended.

I am grateful for the many people who debated with me about democracy during the course of a series of presentations I gave on populism in Belgium, England, Holland, Hungary, Poland, Romania and Sweden since that fateful night in Amsterdam in June 2018. Numerous colleagues at the Twenty First Century Institute in Budapest and elsewhere have provided me with useful criticism. Dr Jennie Bristow, Mick Hume and Jacob Furedi made valuable criticisms and suggestions about the presentation of my arguments.

May 2020

Chapter 1

Introduction – Democracy facing lockdown

Dare I say it, but as I write this under the shadow of the Covid-19 virus, I feel far more anxious about society's estrangement from the ideals of freedom and democracy than about this pandemic's threat to human health. For weeks now, numerous commentators have been questioning whether or not liberal democracies can adequately protect their people. Some even insist that authoritarian states like China are far more able to respond to catastrophes than democracies. Indeed, many make the calculated claim that people's lives are far more precious than the freedom of individuals. Comment articles with titles like 'Can democracy survive the coronavirus?' are now the norm, hinting at the possibility of a future where people's desire for freedom will give way to an outlook dominated by the imperative of survival. 'We need Big Brother to beat this virus', comments a journalist in *The Times*[1].

Of course, friends of democracy are doing their best to fight back. They are rightly concerned about the locking down of democracy and the suspension of hard-won freedoms and rights under the guise of emergency powers. In many nations, parliaments have been suspended, powers of arrest and detention have been expanded and a citizen's right to free movement limited to their home.

No doubt some of these extraordinary measures are necessary to protect communities from the merciless ravages of a pandemic. However, what was, and continues to be, particularly disturbing is not the implementation of emergency powers but the near-total absence of debate on the necessity for these measures and their implications for the future of a free society. Chancellor Angela Merkel of Germany fatalistically described the pandemic as an 'affront to democracy because it restricts our existential rights and needs'[2]. Yet this 'affront to democracy' was not the deed of a virus but of governments who were all too willing to trade in freedom for the promise of safety in a lockdown.

In the UK, where I live, it was the media that led the way in demanding a stringent lockdown. But rather than be ignored and ridiculed by the general population – as so often happens when the media class gets itself in a huff – this sentiment resonated throughout society. Within days, a mood of helplessness and passivity set in. And in turn, its one-dimensional regard for government as the solution to everything soon called into question the foundation on which democracy rests: the role of an active citizen.

As Covid panic gripped the Western world, you could be forgiven for thinking that we were merely pawns in a dystopian thought experiment designed by the seventeenth-century English philosopher Thomas Hobbes. For it is in Hobbes' writings that we find the first systematic attempt to harness people's fear for their lives to promote the proposition that there is no alternative but to exchange freedom for the protection of the state.

In his classic text *The Leviathan*, Hobbes justified an absolutist sovereign on the grounds that his authority was based on his citizens' prior willingness to exchange their liberty for the guarantee of security. Much in the way there has been little kick-back against Covid-19-related emergency rule – all of which is justified in the name of security and health – Hobbes' politics of fear sought to discourage people from adopting an active orientation in the world.

Indeed, one of the principle objectives of his politics of fear was to neutralise the impulse towards risk-taking and social experimentation. He wrote that people had to be persuaded that 'the less they dare, the better it is for both commonwealth and for themselves'. For Hobbes, a stable state discourages its members from living freely.

Now and again I hear twenty-first century soulmates of Hobbes denouncing people who 'dare' to question the advice of experts or the emergency rules enacted in response to Covid-19. Quick to brand anyone who speaks out as a dangerous heretic, they revel in hounding people who take their liberty seriously to give up their individual freedoms 'for the good of their community'.

Typically, this attempt to juxtapose individual freedom with the good of the community in a time of crisis is utterly misleading. For as the history of disasters shows, community solidarity coexists with individuals exercising their judgement, making choices about how to respond to difficult circumstances and assuming responsibility for others through taking the initiative.

Back in 1932, the US Supreme Court Justice Louis Brandeis suggested that we regard local communities as 'laboratories of democracy', where people can experiment and work out solutions to the challenges they face[3]. Research on pandemics and disasters indicates that the ability of individuals to act freely is essential for creative thinking, flexibility and the ability to improvise in newly emergent situations[4].

As I shall explore further in this book, democracy is not a value to be followed and used only when things are looking rosy. Democracy is not just for Christmas. In fact, the very nature of rigorous public debate and participation endows communities with the strength and means to survive pandemics and uncertainty. Contrary to the pessimistic version of freedom peddled by Hobbes, a democratic way of life is far more likely to protect people's lives than an authoritarian regime. It will certainly enhance the quality of those people's lives.

Of course, the ease with which democratic life was put on hold in response to Covid was not simply caused by the fear and insecurity provoked by the threat from this virus. From the turn of the twenty-first century onwards, the political establishment has become increasingly concerned about the apparent loss of its authority. In numerous elections and referenda, the public rejected the advice of the traditional political parties and voted for movements who were outside the mainstream. Especially after the vote for Brexit, a kind of Democracy Panic set in among the political elites. In the present conjuncture, this anti-populist panic constitutes the greatest threat to representative democracy and the flourishing of a democratic culture.

For some time now democracy has ceased to inspire influential opinion formers of Western societies. On university campuses, the value of free and open debate – the very embodiment of a free-thinking, democratic society – is frequently challenged by members of the student and academic community who regard it with contempt. Meanwhile, surveys indicate that in the United States and the United Kingdom only around 30 per cent of the younger voters believe that it is 'essential' to live in a democracy. Covid did not cause the all too apparent estrangement of the Western world from the value of democracy, it merely exposed the fragile foundation on which it rested. The ascendancy of Cancel Culture indicates that a significant section of society views free speech and democracy with contempt.

An anti-democratic moment

Since its emergence in ancient Athens over 2500 years ago, democracy has consistently been threatened by powerful enemies of freedom and equality. Noticeably during the past century – during the 1930s and 1940s – the campaign against democracy assumed the character of a full-blown military conflict. But in the recent era, opponents of democracy have sought to belittle it using a different tactic: by depriving it of its moral authority. For the most part, they do this by calling into question the capacity of people to play the role of an intelligent and responsible citizen. Critics frequently contend that everyday citizens not only lack the knowledge but are also far too irrational to be able to make sound choices.

And so, unlike in the past – in the 1930s, say – today's propaganda war against democracy assumes a *silent* form. Indeed, its silence is almost intrinsic to it – principally because since the end of World War II, it is widely recognised that no regime can possibly claim to be legitimate unless it can assert that its authority rests on public consent and democratic institutions. Even such a sceptic and foe of real democracy as the dictatorial government of North Korea feels obliged to call itself the Democratic Republic of North Korea.

Yet in practice, even in Western liberal democracies it often seems that there is little genuine love for democracy. This sentiment is most strikingly communicated in the mainstream's hostility to movements it describes as populist. The term populist is often used as a term of abuse. Yet it refers to people who simply aspire to gain a voice in public life. In recent years, the electoral success of populist movements and causes has led elite policy-makers and commentators to voice anxiety about the fragility of democratic decision-making. In many cases – at least among the anti-populist commentators and elites – the previous begrudged acceptance of democracy has given way to Democracy Panic.

Don't just take my word for it. Go to any large bookshop and you will find one recently published book after another attacking and criticising democracy. Since the publication of Jason Brennan's invective against the people – *Against Democracy* (2006) – there has been a veritable renaissance in the publication of elitist, anti-democratic tomes.

In recent years, scepticism towards the value of democracy has mutated into outright condemnation in response to the failure of anti-populist interests to make headway in recent elections. For the philosopher A.C. Grayling, the author of *Democracy and its Crisis* (2017), the results of the referendum over Brexit and the result of the 2016 American Presidential Election serve as proof that 'something has gone seriously wrong in the state of democracy'[5].

Grayling is far from alone in condemning democracy for allowing populist movements to make significant headway. Steven Levitsky and Daniel Ziblatt's book *How Democracies Die* (2018) points to 'democratic backsliding', which apparently 'begins at the ballot box'. In this and other studies, democracies' defects are attributed to the unpredictable and irrational behaviour of the people. The coupling of democracy with the metaphor of death is also highlighted in a feature of *Foreign Affairs*, which has as its title; 'Is Democracy Dying?' Books with titles such as *Saving Democracy From Suicide, Democracy In Chains* and *How Democracy Ends*[6] communicate a dystopian sense of foreboding about democracy, based on what they regard as its inability to deliver the right results

On a more fundamental level, this current wave of anti-populist and anti-democratic literature is underpinned by a profound sense of anxiety about the loss of elite authority. Yet its authors consistently fail to acknowledge that this authority has been unravelling ever since the Cold War. The literature communicating Democracy Panic rarely asks itself why representatives of the political establishment struggle to challenge and neutralise the appeal of its populist opponents. Rather than explore the implications of the loss of its authority, they find it much easier to point the finger of blame elsewhere; namely, at the moral deficiencies of voters. The belief that drives Democracy Panic is the conviction that the people cannot be trusted. They are derided and blamed for failing to act in accordance with the wisdom of their political and cultural superiors. As one commentator asserted in *The Atlantic*; 'our most pressing political problem today is that the country abandoned the establishment, not the other way around'[7].

Invariably the pejorative framing of those who abandoned their political superiors leads to the questioning of the value of popular sovereignty and consent. Finding a way of limiting the need for consent has become a key ambition of the political establishment. As we note in Chapter 9, taking policy decision-making out of the realm of politics and shifting it to the domain of technocracy is the favoured tactic used to by-pass the consent of the electorate.

The main reason for writing this book is to show that democracy is under threat. Not like it was in the 1930s, however, when it was subjected to the whims of explicitly authoritarian and totalitarian forces. Instead, it is now victim to a far less crystallised, far more cynical culture of animosity towards the belief that ordinary citizens can be trusted to rule themselves and their society. Indeed, through its representation in the media and within institutions of culture and education, democracy has become entirely associated with negative characteristics – so much so that we are now experiencing a heightened version of what the social commentator Christopher Lasch once characterised as a 'democratic malaise'[8].

Begrudged at best

Since its emergence in ancient Greece, democracy has always been the target of powerful forces who regard the exercise of people's power with dread. But while democracy has been reviled by certain powers for centuries, it could not be erased as those very same leaders were fully aware that they could not govern without, at the very least, the passive consent of the 'many'. Of course, the necessity for consent was from the first only begrudgingly accepted. Indeed, the ruling classes have repeatedly sought ways of limiting the meaning of popular consent, as well as the opportunities for participating in the running of society.

There were two main reasons why, despite all the odds, the aspiration for democracy and popular representation has survived and continues to serve as a source of inspiration. Historically, emperors and monarchs justified their authority by claiming that they personified and represented God's will. But with the passing of time, thanks in part to the move towards secularisation following the Protestant Reformation, justification based on religion lost its power to legitimate the authority of divine kingship. And as I have pointed out elsewhere, since the eighteenth century, rulers have insisted that their status was based on their capacity to represent and express popular opinion[9].

Crucially, the resulting debate about the meaning of popular opinion provided an occasion to widen opportunities for individuals and for groups to voice their views. Kings and nobles could no longer claim to possess a monopoly on political representation. It was in this context that ideas about the right of the people to enjoy greater political influence gained force. And once the genie of popular representation was let out of the bottle, it was only a matter of time before the spirit of democracy gained power and influence.

As we shall explore in the chapters to follow, throughout most of history, democracy was a negative euphemism for the *tyranny of the majority*. Indeed, even after the establishment of representative democracies in the nineteenth century, the capacity of citizens to contribute to the process of decision-making was regarded with scepticism. Throughout the twentieth century, the political life of the West was punctuated with anxiety about the unpredictable consequence of the working of democracy. The fact that democracy has acquired positive connotations is mainly due to the tragic events surrounding the Second World War, and the visceral reaction of humanity to the war's totalitarian violence.

And yet in post-1945 Europe, supporters of representative government were explicitly hostile to the rule of the majority – majoritarian democracy – and relied on technocratic institutions to limit the influence of the electorate. In practice, a rhetorical affirmation of democracy coexisted with a commitment to contain its influence.

This paradox was implicitly recognised even by the American political commentator Francis Fukuyama in his famous celebratory essay on the demise of the Cold War. Pointing to the erosion of explicitly authoritarian alternatives, he remarked that there is no ideology 'with pretensions to universality that is in the position to challenge liberal democracy', adding that there was 'no universal principle of legitimacy other than the sovereignty of the people'[10]. Fukuyama acknowledged that democracy constitutes the only foundation for authority and concluded that 'even non-democrats will have to speak the language of democracy in order to justify their deviation from the single universal standard'.

Fortunately, it is relatively straightforward to spot an anti-democrat in disguise. More often than not, their only justification for putting up with democracy rests upon their cynical observation that all the other alternative narratives have been discredited. And yet for all their half-baked attempts to conceal their genuine anti-democratic convictions, their scorn always lurks in the background, often taking the form of a condescending suspicion towards populism. They use the term populism as a code for communicating the fear that it is a disease of democracy. As one study points out, 'many authors maintain that populism is first and foremost a democratic disease or pathology'[11].

Democracy needs to be upheld as a value in its own right otherwise it will serve instrumental needs and lack inspirational content. Unfortunately, the idea that democracy is valuable in its own right is challenged by the prevailing consensus that regards it merely as a useful instrument for arriving at decisions. It suggests that 'equal right to vote has no intrinsic value'[12]. In Western societies, supporters of liberal democracy argue that liberalism trumps the value of democracy. Fareed Zakaria, a leading critic of populist democracy, explicitly endorses the idea that liberalism is logically superior to democracy. He contends that democracy is about procedures to select a government, whereas liberalism is about the promotion of goals such as the protection of individual autonomy, individual liberty and constitutionalism[13]. According to this schema, liberalism is endowed with a normative content, whereas democracy possesses only procedural qualities.

As we shall see, I take a view that is the direct opposite of Zakaria. To understand why, we must first appreciate that how we view democracy depends on how we regard human beings and their potential for development, for exercising self-rule and for taking responsibility for their community and fellow human beings. For anti-democrats, most humans lack the moral and intellectual resources necessary to trust them with determining the future direction of their society. But from where I see it, to put it simply, it is only through living democratically that people develop their potential to become authors of their own lives and create a society based on genuine solidarity. But more on that later...

Festering in the own self-regard of its proponents, anti-democratic sentiments have acquired the character of a veritable ideology; one that presents itself as a holier-than-thou response to the alleged threat of fascism, xenophobia and the politics of hate. And yet, for all their social media posts about 'solidarity' and 'empowerment', the anti-populist outlook promoted by the Western cultural and political establishment is driven by a profound sense of mistrust and hostility towards democracy and the demos.

To understand the danger this mindset poses to the fabric of democracy, as well as how to combat it, it is necessary to explore the different forms assumed by anti-democratic sentiments throughout the ages.

As ever, we shall begin by returning to ancient Athens, the birthplace of democracy and also, paradoxically, the fountain from which anti-democratic theories originate. The chapters that follow will look at the different forms assumed by the war against democracy through the ages. And we shall finally end our discussion by explaining why democracy is valuable in and of itself, why it's not a means to an end but a way of life that is necessary for human flourishing and development. If there's one lesson to be learned from the global response to Covid-19, it's that we need more democracy. Not less.

Chapter 2

The discovery of democracy

It was in Athens, ancient Greece, that humanity first began to adopt ideas, attitudes and forms of behaviour that eventually became associated with democracy. Philosophers or political theorists did not invent democracy: on the contrary, most were terrified by the prospect of a full-on form of direct democracy, where every citizen could have their say. As this chapter indicates, the war against democracy was launched a long time before the ideals of democracy were integrated into a coherent political outlook.

The values that are integral to the democratic tradition emerged step by step. Athenian citizens did not possess a blueprint that they could follow or implement but learned to become democratic through striving to gain influence over the exercise of political power and acquiring the right to voice their views. As one important study of this development explains, the ordinary people of Athens became free, politically equal and secure because 'by their own actions, they had come to realise that they could be so, and because they were willing, in word and deed, to defend these pragmatic conditions of existence against internal and external threats'[1]. They inspired others to share the belief that rule by the people or *demokratia* was both possible and necessary for the well-being of their community.

Most accounts of Athenian democracy highlight its important institutional features: and to be sure, through participation in the assembly and the courts, Athenian citizens had a direct say in the community's laws and rules, giving democracy real meaning. More importantly, however, the attitudes that we now associate with democracy caught the imagination of a significant section of society; the citizens of Athens actually *lived* democracy.

The democratic spirit was often captured in poems and plays that call into question traditional claims about the supposed superiority of nobles and aristocrats. That Athens eventually allowed the poor to gain political power could not have occurred unless its people questioned the moral authority of the noble and the wealthy. This sentiment was powerfully expressed in Euripides' *Electra* (413 BC), where Orestes declares that 'true nobility and courage lie in character, not bloodline or wealth'[2]. The sentiments expressed by Euripides communicated the important democratic insight that people should be judged by their character rather than their inherited status or wealth. There are numerous examples in Greek literature, where the practical skills and virtues of the people are favourably contrasted to the ostentatious qualities of aristocratic life[3].

The invention of *demokratia*

The word *demokratia* is a synthesis of *demos* and *kratos*. The term *demos* conveys the idea of ordinary, even poor citizens of the city-state, taking seriously the idea that it is they who should possess the power to rule. The term *kratos* is best interpreted as power or control, and when used in combination with demos, *demokratia* referred to a system of government where ordinary citizens possessed political power and could therefore participate in the making of decisions that affected their city-state. Originally, *demokratia* referred to people's capacity to do things to bring about change through collective decision-making[4].

In the first instance, the construction of the term 'democracy' should be interpreted as a linguistic recognition that a significant section of Athenian citizens during the fifth century BC regarded themselves as free and politically equal citizens. Such sentiments were expressed through speech acts and forms of behaviour indicating an aspiration to possess rights of citizens, who were politically equal with the wealthy and aristocratic members of their community.

The discovery of democracy could only have occurred in a culture that took politics seriously. And indeed, as Thornton notes, 'The Greeks recognized that the conception of human flourishing – the achievement of virtue and the good life, which in turn create happiness – was dependent on living "politically"'[5]. 'The goal of politics is the good for humans,' stated the philosopher Aristotle. Politics, which could only be exercised in the public arena of a city-state, served as an invitation for citizens to take public life seriously. It also created a demand for participation and voice.

Even before the invention of the word *demokratia*, the political culture of Athens upheld the value of *isegoria*, which referred to the 'equality of all citizens in the right to speak in the governing assembly'. Along with *isegoria*, the Athenians also valued *insomnia*, which referred to the principle of equality before the law[6]. The significance of this principle was that 'it promised the poorest citizen an equal right in law-making, law administering, law enforcing power of the state'[7]. More than 2500 years later, we have learned that the equality of citizens before the law is the most important guarantor of justice. The possession of equal rights to address an assembly, along with the right to equal treatment before the law, indicated that the political culture of Athens was relatively open to the institutionalisation of political equality. According to one study, democratic knowledge and behaviour was created and recreated through the 'collective practices of public communication' rather 'than being given by an external authority or discovered through intellectual effort'[8].

The single most important legacy of Athenian democracy was the idealisation of political equality. Integral to this conception of citizenship was the belief that regardless of their social or economic position, all citizens possessed the capacity and the judgement to manage the institutions of the state. This point was well made by Athens' political leader Pericles in his famous *Funeral Oration*:

Advancement in public life falls to reputation for capacity, class considerations not being allowed to interfere with merit; nor again does poverty bar the way, if a man is able to serve the state, he is not hindered by the obscurity of his condition[9].

One important illustration of how Athens acted on this belief was the practice of sortation. Most public offices in Athens were sortive, filled at random by a lottery of citizens, and the jurors who presided over key cases and participated in the making of Athenian law were chosen from a panel of 6000 citizens by lot each year.

Through a gradual process of attempting to find their political voice, the citizens of Athens thus discovered democracy. Political experimentation, and citizens' aspiration for influence and power, created the conditions for the crystallisation of the idea of *demokratia*. Researchers and historians have been unable to discover surviving texts 'written with the explicit intention of explaining to a reader the principles on which Athenian democracy was predicated'[10] – and it is unlikely that such a text ever existed, as democracy evolved slowly through customs that, by their very nature, could not be synthesised into a settled ideology. Although a new form of people power acquired a powerful presence in Athens, it lacked an ideology or philosophy that could validate it.

The birth of anti-democratic thought

Paradoxically, most of what we know about Greek democracy comes from the statements of its opponents. The wealthy oligarchy that traditionally ruled Athens could never reconcile itself to the political influence of the *demos*, and regarded the city-states' democratically-inspired customs, laws and institutions with hostility. The wresting of political power by the people swiftly led to the formulation of anti-democratic theories and polemics, which emerged a long time before the formulation of a coherent democratic outlook.

By the middle of the fifth century BC, opponents of the *demos* argued that what democracy really meant was the tyranny of the mob: 'the domination of the many poor over the wealthy few'[11]. Some sources have gone so far as to claim that the word 'democracy' was coined by its enemies as a term to decry the behaviour of the *demos*. While the authorship of this word continues to be a matter of debate, at least within elite philosophical and intellectual discourse, the usage of the term democracy communicated negative characteristics.

The most important and influential attack on democracy was penned by the philosopher Plato. In *The Republic*, Plato advanced a systematic critique of the rule of the many and portrayed democracy as a form of mob rule that inevitably paved the way for tyranny. In his numerous dialogues, he highlighted the selfish, irrational and brutal characteristics of the Athenian mob by blaming them for the death of his hero, the philosopher Socrates. This exposed the anxiety with which the Greek elites regarded the attempt of the *demos* to participate within, and control, the political institutions of their city-state.

Western political theory itself was born as a response to the threat posed by democracy. Greek political theory was devoted to the task of discrediting and marginalising claims supporting democratic customs, institutions and practices. As one study on the history of the 'mob' observes, 'it could almost be said that political theorizing was *invented* to show that democracy, the rule of men by themselves, necessarily turns into rule by the mob'. John McClelland, the author of this study, argues that the Western tradition of political thought 'begins with this profoundly anti-democratic bias'[12]. The elite's criticism of Athenian democracy was promoted systematically and led to the formulation of the first coherent elaboration of political theory. As we shall see these criticisms continue to influence Democracy Panic to this day.

The spirit of democracy

The practice of democracy in Athens was far from perfect. For a start, political life was restricted to adult male citizens, who made up around 20 per cent of the population: women, non-citizens and slaves were excluded. Restrictions on the exercise of political rights were paralleled by a narrow and place-specific conception of the meaning of freedom and equality. Humanity lacked a concept of universality, and people's customs and practices were perceived as applying to themselves and their community. It was from this local and particularist perspective that Athenians understood their own political culture. Consequently, the Athenian conception of democracy was not linked to an ideal of freedom and equality that applied universally to all people.

In the current era, critics of the achievements of Greek civilisation dwell on the shortcomings of Athenian democracy, rather than its achievements. The Greeks are condemned for their ethnocentrism, for practising slavery and for oppressing women and their ethnocentrism. The tendency to question the significance of the discovery of democracy more than 2500 years ago reflects a narrow-minded practice of judging the past according to the standards of our times. In this way, twenty-first century critics of ancient Greece flatter themselves about how much more aware they are now.

When history is simply read backwards, the distinctive features of human experience become flattened out. Critics overlook the fact that what was distinctive and special about Athenian democracy was not its treatment of slaves and women, since communities throughout the Ancient World possessed similar attitudes and practices. What was distinctive about Athens was that its people discovered democracy and realised that it should be the many, rather than the few, who should rule society. The democracy of Athens was limited and incomplete, but once people became interested in assuming control over their political institutions, it was only a matter of time before others would follow suit.

The contemporary notion of human equality owes a debt of gratitude to Athenian citizens, because they developed an idea of political citizenship that was based on the principle that all citizens – regardless of their wealth – were equally competent and entitled to participate in the affairs of the state. As citizens, everyone was equal before the law. This was the first time in human history where the ideal of equality – albeit in a limited sense – was institutionalised. Athens took the first gigantic step on the road of the age-old struggle for real equality. Once equality was seen as a positive virtue for some, it was only a matter of time before it became seen as an important possession for humanity as a whole.

Why Athens?

Discussions of Athenian democracy often focus on its institutional practices – the functioning of this city-state's assembly, courts and administration. But while these institutions were important, what is more significant is the spirit of democracy and the cultural attitudes and practices that motivated the behaviour of the *demos*. At its best, democracy is a lived experience that animates people to participate actively in the running of their government. To understand why this powerful sentiment captured the imagination of the people of Athens, it is important to understand its unique cultural drivers.

Unlike the ancient civilisations of the Mediterranean and the Middle East, the Greek city-states were far less dominated by a centralised system of administration. The people of Greece enjoyed greater latitude for developing and altering their customs than their counterparts in other societies. In contrast to the Egyptian or Hebrew cultures, the Greeks did not have a centrally coordinated and organised religion: there were numerous cults, and the Greeks lacked a single orthodoxy of belief. Greek culture was therefore unusually argumentative and open to the idea of discussion and debate, and provided opportunities for people to question its customs, religion and tradition[13].

The dynamic philosophical culture of Greece, along with its impressive intellectual developments in science, was greatly assisted by its impressive culture of literacy. According to Jack Goody and Ian Watt, writing facilitated the development of abstract thought[14]. Goody and Watt claimed that the rise of literacy provided the cultural foundation for the development of science and philosophy in ancient Greece, and that furthermore, 'alphabetic reading and writing was probably an important consideration in the development of political democracy in Greece'[15].

Free citizens of Greece could read laws and play an informed role in public life. The written codification of cultural tradition 'brought about an awareness of two things: of the past as different from the present; and of the inherent inconsistencies in the picture of life as it was inherited by the individual from the cultural tradition in its recorded form'[16]. The ability to perceive inconsistencies encouraged the attitude of questioning, which in turn fostered a disposition towards critical thought. This extraordinary critical spirit helped foster a climate where the politics of democracy could prosper.

Athenian society was also uniquely oriented towards change and seizing opportunities. A community oriented towards change is unlikely to be dominated by an ethos that insists on blind obedience and respect for the customs and traditions of the past. In such a community authority and officialdom is held in scant esteem, let alone awe. One consequence of this irreverent attitude towards authority is the relative absence of formal institutions and hierarchical structures. It is not entirely clear whether bold, risk-taking sentiments led to Athens' democratic political culture or whether it was the other way around. However, in a world where authority was to a limited extent open to question, individuals are less likely to see themselves as inferior to others. In such circumstances, ideas about right and wrong are not communicated through the received wisdom of tradition but are crystallised through discussion and debate with others. And when the views and opinions of others become important, a more argumentative and democratic political culture can emerge.

Political fluidity and instability was an integral part of Athenian culture, and its disposition to change encouraged a democratic ethos which, in turn, made it difficult to consolidate and institutionalise social and political hierarchies. This created continuous problems for those seeking to institutionalise the power of the elite.

Athenian society worked most of the time because its people identified with their city. This was a community where authority was invested in the people and the opinions they expressed through the Athenian assembly and other public venues. The legitimacy enjoyed by public opinion and its democratic culture was reinforced by historical events, such as the defeat of the Persians by the Athenian navy at the Battle of Salamis. The poor sailors of the Athenian navy, rather than heroic upper-class warriors, were identified with the glory of Athens. The victory at Salamis 'helped open the public arena in both size and substance beyond anything known in the Hellenic world by legitimating the claims to power and authority of the poor whose courage and steadfastness had won the victory[17]'.

Openness to new experience, an argumentative disposition and valuation of literacy and education provided the unique cultural terrain on which democratic attitudes could flourish. The cultural attitudes that prevailed deprived the elites of the intellectual and moral resources necessary for legitimating oligarchical political rule. The insecurity of the Athenian elites and the difficulty they had in converting their superior economic position into unquestioned political authority provided an opportunity for the demos to gain significant rights and power. In these unique circumstances, democracy made its first – albeit hesitant and temporary – appearance.

The energy fuelling Athens' democratic culture was its critical spirit, most dramatically exhibited through the authority of debating and arguing. Speaking freely was and remains the foundation of democracy. 'Freemen have free tongues,' stated Sophocles. As Thornton reminds us, 'in Athens the right of free and equal political speech at the heart of political freedom and justice, constituted one of the essential attributes of citizenship'[18]. The aspiration for, and realisation of, a voice by the citizens of Athens gave life to democracy. Today, when 40 per cent of young Americans between the ages of 18-43 support censoring speech that is offensive to others, it is evident that a democratic argumentative culture is in trouble[19]. When many members of the Western educational and cultural establishment prefer to emphasise the problems with freedom of speech rather than its virtues, it is important to remind ourselves of the legacy of Athens and remember that once this freedom becomes devalued, democracy loses its critical spirit.

The recurring themes in the war against democracy

From the outset, opponents of democracy argued that free speech and the open circulation of ideas was a curse. For example, Plato did not believe that public discussion and debate assisted clarification and enlightenment. In his *Gorgias*, he argues that public speechmaking has no redeeming features. As Ober explains, Plato argued that public speech 'caters indiscriminately to the desires of the many (thereby corrupting them) while simultaneously serving to corrupt the speaker and to enslave him to the multitude'[20].

Plato, along with members of the Greek oligarchy, distrusted the multitude and regarded them as a mob that had to be controlled rather than reasoned with. He rejected the idea that the *demos* could be educated through discussion and debate and he repudiated the idea that the multitude could discriminate between good and bad ideas. He was troubled by the spread of literacy, in part because he feared that written ideas had the potential to acquire a life of their own. He asserted that writing is indiscriminate in that it 'roams about everywhere': it does not discern between readers who can understand and benefit from its communication, and those who will become misled and confused by it.

Speaking through the mouth of Socrates, Plato warned that writing reaches those with 'understanding no less than those who have no business with it'[21]. In line with his paternalistic worldview, he assumed that in the wrong hands a little knowledge was a threat to social order. From Plato's outlook, those who had no business reading the written word were the vast majority of the public, the uneducated *demos*. From his perspective, even words of wisdom could, when written down, serve as a catalyst for confusion. Plato observed that problems would occur if the questions raised by a written manuscript were not dealt with in the presence of someone with wisdom.

In today's self-consciously inclusive democratic public culture, the inclination to restrict people's freedom to read material of their own choosing would be seen as anathema. Yet, even in the twenty-first century, the public are often represented as powerless victims of media manipulation by tabloid journalism or by the subliminal techniques of advertisers. The conviction that the masses cannot be trusted to discriminate between good and bad ideas and are likely to be confused and manipulated by the media is an enduring feature of anti-democratic thought.

Plato's reflection on censorship and reading was underpinned by a powerful sense of mistrust of the moral and intellectual capacities of the *demos*. This reaction was based on what constitutes the most durable feature of the anti-democratic ethos: the belief that because of their mental and moral deficits, the people have no role to play in the administration and government of political life.

Discourses that sought to contrast the mental deficiencies of the many to the virtues of the few became commonplace towards the end of the fifth century BC in response to the growing political influence of the demos. In *Crito*, Socrates rejects Crito's concern with the ideas of the many on the grounds that they are 'only the doctrines of the multitude, who would be as ready to restore people to life, if they were able, as they are to put them to death – and with as little reason'[22].

Arguably, it was Plato's Socrates who provided one of the earliest critiques of what today is referred to as populism. He was preoccupied by the authority enjoyed by the *demos*, and argued that it lacked the expertise and judgement required for governing a city-state. Socrates was convinced that politics was the business, not of the people, but of experts. In his dialogue with Protagoras, Socrates complained that when it comes to constructing a building or a ship, the community relies on expert architects or shipwrights, yet when it comes to the administration of the state every citizen is allowed to have an equal voice. He added that 'when it is something to do with the government of the country that is to be debated, the man who gets up to advise them may be a builder or equally well a blacksmith or a shoemaker, a merchant or ship owner, rich or poor, of good family or none'[23].

Socrates was in no doubt that 'what most people think' on political matters is far less important than the views of the one man who really understands the issues at stake – the expert[24]. If not the expert, who will exercise authority over the *demos*? This was a question that was formulated a long time before the emergence of the current anti-populist cultural script. The conviction that the people are morally and intellectually inferior to their enlightened superiors constitutes the historical foundation of the anti-populist imagination. Throughout most of human history it was through the anti-populist accounts of philosophers and writers like Plato that people learned about the experience of the Athenian *demos*. That is why for centuries, Athenian democracy was regarded as a negative experience to be avoided at all costs.

Plato's claim that democracy inevitably leads to tyranny is constantly recycled in twenty-first century anti-populist narratives. In an influential essay, titled 'Democracies end when they are too democratic', Andrew Sullivan cites the warning of Plato regarding the inevitability of democracy mutating into tyranny[25]. In a voice of despair, he noted that it is 'hard not to see in Plato's vision a murky reflection of our own hyperdemocratic times'. In current times, the refrain that '2400 years ago, Plato saw democracy would give rise to a tyrannical leader' is frequently repeated by those overwhelmed by the sensibility of Democracy Panic[26].

Chapter 3

The slow and painful emergence of the democratic ideal

In her essay 'What is Freedom', the political philosopher Hannah Arendt wrote of 'the miracle of freedom's rare appearance'[1]. This should serve as a warning against the inclination to take democracy for granted. Looking back on the experience of the past two thousand years, it is evident that democracy has had a rare and precarious existence. Very few philosophers, theologians and political leaders have historically endorsed the belief that a government based on the people is the best form of political rule. Even in recent decades, more intellectual energy is devoted to finding faults with democracy than with celebrating it.

The practice of democratic citizenship that entitles people to political equality more or less vanished until the eighteenth century. Until the modern era, people were mostly relegated to the role of subjects of their rulers, rather than citizens. In the rare circumstances where political citizenship meant something – for example, the Roman Empire – it did not imply that people enjoyed equal political rights. Although the American and French revolutions of the eighteenth century began to give real meaning to citizenship, genuine democratic practice had to wait until the twentieth century.

Hobbes' dilemma

During the centuries following the rise of democracy in Athens, the world only heard about this momentous political experiment through the mouths of its naysayers. In the Western world, political and religious authorities regarded democracy as either an outrage or a major threat to order and civilisation. The demos was usually depicted as a mob, whose irrational and violent behaviour invariably led to the usurpation of power by a tyrant. In most commentaries, the rule of the many in Athens was described as a force of evil[2].

The attitude held by seventeenth-century English philosopher Thomas Hobbes, the founder of modern political philosophy and a major contributor to the development of liberalism, typified early modernity's view of the problem posed by people's aspiration for a voice. Hobbes was haunted by the spectre of Athens. He, like the vast majority of his contemporary European thinkers, regarded democracy as a dangerous and destructive force. In 1629, he translated Thucydides's *History of the Peloponnesian War* with the aim of demonstrating the evils of democracy. Hobbes noted that Thucydides' hostility to democracy 'was in part what made him worthy of translation'[3].

Hobbes' commitment to de-legitimating democracy was not merely motivated by his philosophical and intellectual interests. Europe, and England in particular, was going through a protracted period of social upheaval and civil and religious strife. Soon after the publication of his warning against the folly of democracy, the English Civil War broke out. For a time, this led to an unprecedented explosion of people's power, as the radical Levellers' demands echoed some of the aspirations of the Athenian *demos*. Among these demands were universal male suffrage, equality before the law, biennial elections and religious tolerance. It was the desire to pre-empt, contain and ultimately crush radical movements like the Levellers that motivated Hobbes to put pen to paper.

The Levellers were not the first post-Athenian movement to express an ambition for the realisation of a measure of equality. For example, the Peasants' Revolt by Wat Tyler in England, 1381, anticipated the aspiration of modern democratic movements for freedom and equality. John Ball, one of this rebellion's leaders, was excommunicated by the Church for his sermons advocating a classless society. His words to the rebels at Blackheath Common – 'When Adam dug and Eve span, who was then the gentleman?' – resonate with the democratic populist imagination to this day.. However, the leaders of the Peasants' Revolt were not able to transform their aspiration for equality into a coherent, democratically-inspired outlook.

It was not until the English Civil War that the ideals and aspirations associated with *demokratia* re-emerged as a focus for political mobilisation. Although the Levellers were soon crushed, their experience provided an example on which numerous radical democratic movements would draw in the centuries to come. As Mick Hume writes:

> the first directly elected body in England was formed not in the aristocratic atmosphere of the Westminster parliament or some local parish council but within the rank and file of Oliver Cromwell's New Model Army[4].

The Levellers outraged the powers-that-be when one of their leaders, Colonel Thomas Rainsborough MP, asserted that the poor had the right to consent to the system of government under which they lived. He argued that the 'poorest man in England is not at all bound in a strict sense to the government that he hath not had a voice to put himself under'[5]. Neither Rainsborough nor the other leaders used the term 'democracy' to refer to their objective, but they introduced its foundational principles to the modern world.

The political and cultural conditions that prevailed in the decades leading up to and during the Civil War resembled those of democratic Athens in one important respect. A critical spirit that encouraged people to ask questions and to argue and debate about the key political issues that confronted them created a form of public life that invited the participation of many people who had hitherto felt unable to raise their voice.

The period saw the dramatic growth of literacy, which had the effect of radicalising public affairs. The emergence of a reading public had a significant impact on the conduct of public affairs. Seventeenth-century England saw a massive increase in the quantity of printed material, from 22 pamphlets published in 1640 to 1966 published in 1642.

Radical Protestant and Puritan sects promoted reading and encouraged their adherents to exercise their individual conscience. At the time, those in authority rightly regarded the call on people to live in accordance with their conscience as a threat to order. This was a dangerous development, wrote the historian Lawrence Stone, because, 'it aroused expectations of political and religious participation and exposed large numbers of humble people to the heady egalitarian wine of the New Testament'[6]. One account of this historical moment describes the 'extraordinary period of freedom as authority withered away'[7], while a study of the politics of literacy in this era states: 'the Civil War, as we know was preceded by a print war, a war of words – and one that the king lost'[8]. The aggregate effect of the widening of debate among the new constituency of readers was the entry of common people into the public life of the nation.

This era also saw a growing opposition to censorship and a demand for free speech. The radical poet and intellectual John Milton was strident in his denunciation of those who questioned the capacity of readers to discriminate between what was right and wrong. The extraordinary confidence that Milton attached to readers' capacity to make reasoned judgements was coupled with his conviction that what caused evil was not the content and arguments contained in the printed text, but the failure to challenge and discredit misguided and corrupt arguments. He criticised the impulse to censor on the grounds that 'knowledge cannot defile, nor consequently the books, if the will and conscience be not defiled'[9]. Readers of virtue would not be corrupted by what they read. Indeed, Milton went so far as to argue that independent readers could learn from having to engage with misguided ideas.

For Milton, reading was directly associated with reasoning, which in turn was intimately intermeshed with judging. In one of the most memorable passages of *Areopagitica*, Milton reminds his audience that when God gave Adam reason, 'he gave him freedom to choose, for reason is but choosing'[10]. His insistence that 'reason is but choosing' provided a powerful argument for the freedom of the press and also offered a moral case for uncensored reading.

Milton's trust in the reader's capacity to reason was underwritten by his confidence in the capacity of people to think for themselves. This confidence in people, which was shared by the radical wing of the Parliamentary forces in England, made possible the rise of the first proto-democratic movement in the modern world. That arguments about the relation between the people and their government now had to be played out in front of an ever-expanding audience of politically interested and literate people would ensure that, in the future, popular consent could rarely be taken for granted.

The English Civil War, leading to the overthrow of the monarchy and the new opportunities created for the widening of participation in public life, meant that it was no longer possible to ignore the aspirations of the people. During the seventeenth century a growing number of commentators came to the conclusion that political rule could only work if it was based on a degree of popular consent. The question of how to establish a form of political authority that could claim to be based on popular consent but not yield power to the people intrigued Hobbes. He drew the conclusion that political rule could only be effective if it could demonstrate that it was based on the consent of those whom it ruled. He concluded that the 'power of the mighty hath no foundation but in the opinion and belief of the people'[11].

Hobbes has a reputation for being a non-apologetic advocate of absolutist authoritarian rule. Certainly, *Leviathan* provides a coherent justification for the necessity of a form of absolute, unquestionable authority. However, his theory was oriented towards resolving the tension between the necessity for a form of absolute, unquestionable authority, and the need to validate political rule with the consent of the ruled. *Leviathan* offered an unambiguous case for an absolute sovereign but it also insisted that the effectiveness of an absolute sovereign was contingent on the capacity to claim the authority provided by consent[12]. His synthesis of the sovereignty of absolute power with the consent of the people was communicated through his notion of a social contract.

Hobbes' Social Contract was based on the premise that, in exchange for individuals giving up some of their personal liberty, the supreme ruler will provide them with protection and security. Hobbes initiated the social contract tradition which was later taken up by John Locke and other liberal philosophers. Hobbes' version of a social contract offered an account of political authority and obligation whose foundation was provided by the consent of the governed. This tradition insisted that political conventions were the product of the voluntary accord of free and equal individuals who willingly gave up their freedom in exchange for the ruler's promise of protecting their lives and their property.

Hobbes' representation of the crystallisation of political authority as a covenant based on people's willingness to exchange their freedom for security offered a coherent attempt to reconcile absolute sovereignty with popular consensus. As one study remarked, Hobbes is 'the most striking example' of an absolutist determined to uphold authority on the basis of popular consent:

> for he set out to accomplish nothing less than a defence of absolutism on the basis of the most democratic principles

current in the revolutionary period. He adopted the radical idiom of natural right, the natural freedom and equality of all individuals (at least all male heads of households), and the doctrine that no principle of nature sanctions the division between ruler and ruled, so that there can be no legitimate authority except that which is ultimately based on consent[13].

What is remarkable about Hobbes' theory is that he appropriated the language and egalitarian principles of English radicalism in order to uphold absolutism and suppress democratic sentiments. Hobbes left no one in doubt that he regarded indivisible authority as the *sine qua non* for the maintenance of order and stability. But he did not worship power for its own sake: he recognised that the obedience of the people could not be gained through coercion alone. His theory also demonstrated that in principle, it was possible to claim the authority of a popular mandate without making the smallest concession to it.

Consent without democracy

Athenian democracy served as a negative example to successive generations of rulers, who were educated into perceiving the political influence of demos as toxic and destructive. Nevertheless, in different epochs it was recognised that the aspirations of the many could not be entirely ignored, and those who held the levers of power often sought to create institutional arrangements that allowed rulers to claim that they ruled by consent. Hobbes was by no means the first philosopher to recognise the importance of associating political authority with consent. The elites of ancient Rome were keen students of the experience of the Greeks, and drew the lesson that although democracy had to be avoided at all costs, there had to be a safety valve through which the people could voice their interests and aspirations.

Until the middle of the second century BC, the Roman

Republic rested on a carefully crafted system of checks and balances. Public life in the city was managed through a system of countervailing influences referred to as a 'mixed constitution', through which power was dispersed and carefully calibrated. This system aimed to minimise the tension between conflicting interests and, in particular, sought to reconcile the plebeian masses to the preservation of a hierarchy dominated by an elite group of aristocrats. Accordingly, the plebeians gained the right to elect their own officers, the people's tribunes, which according to one account 'made the plebs almost a state within the state'. Despite periodic expressions of dissent and even rebellion, the aristocracy was able to retain control over the running of government.

Rome's republican form of government allowed the plebeian masses to express their views through their tribunes without directly threatening the rule of this city-state's oligarchy. Its purpose was to provide all sections of society with a degree of representation without the provision of democratic rights, operating as a safety valve that allowed the people to express their views.

Republican forms of governance were also adopted by Italian city-states, whose aristocratically-dominated governments attempted to gain the consent of all sections of society. Although Republican leaders and theorists recognised that a constitution had to find a place for some form of representation of mass sentiments, they were resolutely anti-democratic. Most of them regarded the poor with contempt and dismissed the views of the masses as unworthy of their interest.

Unlike most Republican theorists, the late Renaissance political philosopher Nicó Machiavelli had an ambiguous attitude towards the masses. At times, his view of the people was one of disdain. He wrote that 'men are so simple, and governed so absolutely by their present needs, that he who wishes to deceive will never fail in finding willing dupes'. But in his *Discourses*, Machiavelli adopted a more positive account of the people and claimed that 'the populace is more prudent, more stable, and of sounder judgement than the prince'[14]. In a chapter titled 'The Multitude Is Wiser and More Constant Than a Prince', Machiavelli concluded that when the multitude is governed by laws, it is no less wise than the ruler.

Machiavelli believed that the state would benefit from the contribution of the masses and was prepared to incorporate them into the institutions of public life. He felt that the people could contain the arbitrary and impulsive behaviour of the ruler, and his proposals provided a space for the conduct of debate and public activity, and a widening sphere of political participation.

Machiavelli was centuries ahead of his time, and his relatively balanced account of the role of the masses was far closer to the ideals of democratic Athens than the new breed of 'democratic' republicans that led the United States to independence in the eighteenth century. Though in 1776, the founding fathers of the United States declared that all men were equal, in reality they were determined to keep at bay any attempt to import the Athenian form of egalitarian democracy to the New World. They were in no doubt that the experience of Athens was one that had to be avoided. One of the Founding Fathers, Alexander Hamilton, warned in 1787 that 'it is impossible to read the history of the petty republics of Greece and Italy without feeling sensations of horror and disgust'[15].

Most of the Founders regarded the rule of the majority as a form of tyranny that threatened the wealthy and the cultured sections of society. Thomas Jefferson, who was to become the third president of the US, allegedly stated that, 'democracy is nothing more than mob rule, where 51 per cent of the people may take away the rights of the other 49%'[16]. John Adams, the second US president, echoed similar sentiments, predicting that democracy would mean that 'the idle, the vicious, the intemperate would rush into the utmost extravagance of debauchery' at the expense of the propertied minority, with the result that 'anarchy and tyranny commence'[17]. James Madison, the fourth president of the US, called democracy the 'most vile form of government'[18]. He portrayed democratic rule as a 'mortal disease'.

What these leading statesmen wanted was a republic based on the election of representatives along with checks and balances that insulated the nation's rulers from popular pressure. They mistrusted the capacity of the people to behave responsibly, and therefore sought to limit its influence on the political system. That is why the Founding Founders rejected the principle of universal suffrage, not only for white women and black slaves, but also for white males. As one commentator notes, the 'fear of "tyranny of the majority" also served as a kind of ideological basis for the United States political system'[19].

Yet the leaders of the American Revolution could not entirely ignore the egalitarian impulses that motivated many of their supporters. They responded to popular pressure by developing an indirect form of democracy, one that combined the electoral principle with that of representation. The first use of the term *representative democracy* was in a letter by Alexander Hamilton – commending the constitution of New York State in 1777[20]. Though this form of democracy provided the people with the right of representation, it assigned a limited role to the citizens. The American Constitution went beyond previous attempts to offer a voice to the people. Through constructing a system of checks and balances it sought to establish a political system that could claim the consent of the people as the foundation for political authority. But though it represented an important step forward in the long road towards representative government, it was still not a genuine democratic statement.

It took nearly 100 years for the ideal of democracy to be rehabilitated, by a movement of republican democrats led by Andrew Jackson, the seventh president of the US and the founder of the Democratic Party in 1828. It is worth noting that the rise of Jacksonian Democracy, which expanded suffrage to most white men over the age of 21, coincided with what numerous commentators described as a 'Greek fever' spreading across to America. 'No longer is the popular regime of ancient Athens intended to frighten, to conjure up images of chaos and disorder, as in *The Federalist Papers*, or in Hobbes,' notes one historian[21]. Ancient Athens now became a symbol of civilisation and culture; and with American democrats celebrating its legacy, democracy was finally beginning to break through the centuries-long ideological quarantine that surrounded it.

The rehabilitation of democracy

In 1789, 13 years after the Declaration of Independence of the United States, the French Revolution broke out. This revolution, with its slogan of *'Liberté, Egalité, Fraternité'*, promoted a mood of unprecedented confidence in people's capacity to assume control over their destiny. This was the moment when democracy was finally reborn, as an ideal that motivated a significant section of society. As one historian notes: 'We must remember that it was only with the French Revolution that the word "democracy" changes from a term laden with negative implications to a term of praise.'[22]

Until the French Revolution, the question of consent was influenced by the pragmatic quest to maintain non-democratic authority. The revolution's Declaration of the Rights of Man and of the Citizen called into question the previous top-down model of consent. It advanced an idea of representative government that enshrined in law the equality of rights of French citizens, and upheld the liberal Enlightenment values of individual rights and the principle of democratic consent. For the first time, the principle of consent had real democratic content, as it conveyed the idea of an agreement made by equals and implicitly contradicted the idea of subordination to a superior. 'The French revolution of 1789 was the principal turning point in the transition from the authority of kings to the mandate of the people,' states the sociologist Reinhardt Bendix[23]. After this point, it became increasingly difficult for anti-democratic leaders to express their point of view openly.

Although the French Revolution eventually unravelled and mutated into the dictatorship and empire of Napoleon, the ideal of democracy could not be entirely extinguished. From this point onwards, the enemies of democracy adopted more subtle and indirect modes of waging a war against it. In the nineteenth century, under mass pressure, governments began to expand the franchise, while creating institutional checks and balances to limit the influence of the *demos*.

In effect the principle of democracy became rehabilitated by detaching it from the influence of the *demos*. By the middle of the nineteenth century, commentators across the political spectrum realised that whether they liked it or not, popular sovereignty would, at least formally, constitute a fundamental principle of politics.

In the 1890s the spirit of democracy was enthusiastically promoted by the newly founded populist movement. The term populist became a nickname for the People's Party, a mass movement seeking social and economic justice. It was at this point in time that the modern form of Democracy Panic kicked in.

Theodore Roosevelt expressed this sentiment when he wrote in his diary that the populists 'should be put up against the wall and shot', since their campaign was nothing less 'than an appeal to the torch'[24].

Anti-populist hysteria was whipped up by the elite controlled media. They were particularly concerned by the attempt of populist organisers to forge unity between white and black farmers in the southern regions of the United States. Newspapers in the South exclaimed that it was 'threatened with anarchy and communism'. This early attempt to achieve racial equality became the target of a venomous campaign of hate by the anti-populist press[25]. Though in the end this movement was defeated, its aims and objectives serve as a source of inspiration to this day.

In most Western societies, the ideal of a democratic public life could not be outwardly repudiated. As Westel Woodbury Willoughby, one of the founders of American political science, stated in 1917:

> The political philosophy of England since 1688 at least, of France since 1789 and of the United States since its foundation, is squarely committed to the proposition that all political authority comes from the people, and is not vested in the rulers as an original or inherent right[26].

This rhetorical affirmation of popular sovereignty was rarely matched by a willingness to expound a genuinely democratic system of political authority. Popular sovereignty was frequently posed as a fact of life that governments had to put up with. However, experience has shown that the claim to represent popular sovereignty often coexists with a profound sense of mistrust towards democracy, especially in its majoritarian form.

Since its rehabilitation, democracy has been tolerated but without much love. Democracy is rarely appreciated as a way of life that best ensures human flourishing. Deprived of its normative content and detached from majoritarian participation, democracy is often seen as merely a technique for choosing representatives. As with Hobbes, democratic consent serves the role of an instrument for providing legitimacy to political authority. It was on this instrumental ground that Grayling argued for the desirability of universal suffrage, when he said: 'I think the answer lies in the justifications one can give for the source of legitimacy in politics and government[27].'

As I discuss in the next chapter, the durability of instrumental

Chapter 4

Fear of the people: Its long legacy

The slow and painful emergence of democracy, and its partial and limited rehabilitation, was the outcome of two historical trends. First, and most importantly, the continual attempts to discredit democracy were closely linked to ruling authorities' determination to protect their power and privileges, and to limit the influence of popular aspiration. Such calculations influence political behaviour to this day. A related source of apprehension, which was shared by virtually all shades of political opinion, was the perception that if people possessed influence and power, it would be used to the detriment of order and stability.

Fear and mistrust of the masses, the tendency to perceive them at worst as a violent mob or at best as incapable of acting rationally, was not confined to hard-line monarchists and reactionaries. Even radical and revolutionary thinkers mistrusted the demos to the point that they were reluctant to extend to them the power of decision-making. Suspicion towards the urban masses and ordinary people was frequently expressed by the leading thinkers associated with the Enlightenment. Although the leaders of the Enlightenment celebrated theirs as an Age of Reason and adopted hopeful and positive views about the role of humans, they held back from including the uneducated and poor majority in their optimistic vision of progress.

That even radical liberal thinkers held such negative views about their social and political inferiors indicates the depth and breadth of mistrust. The influence of this enduring attitude is crucial for understanding Democracy Panic. Even today, the rhetorical affirmation of democracy is often coupled with concern about the capacities of the electorate. Indeed, almost every well-known study of democracy published in recent years qualifies its endorsement of democracy by raising questions about the people's capability for self-rule.

Spinoza's dilemma

The Dutch philosopher Baruch Spinoza stands out as the only seventeenth-century philosopher who adopted a positive orientation towards democracy, to the point where he has been described as 'the first democrat in the history of philosophy'[1]. In this respect, Spinoza was a genuine pioneer. In contrast to the prevailing consensus held by every school of political philosophy at the time, Spinoza held the view that democracy possessed advantages over other forms of rule. His belief in the natural equality of all men provided the normative foundation of his attitude.

Spinoza had another, more instrumental, justification for democracy, in believing that a democratic electorate and assembly provided the safeguard against arbitrary rule. To some extent, Spinoza shared Machiavelli's belief in the wisdom of the masses. In anticipation of the crystallisation of nineteenth-century radical liberal attitudes towards free speech and debate, he argued that a democratic assembly is likely to make sounder decisions than a monarch or an oligarchy because in an assembly, people will make better judgements than if they are making decisions without an opportunity 'to have their wits sharpened by discussing, listening to others, and debating'[2]. He concluded that popular assemblies tend to deliberate and legislate more wisely than more restricted political bodies.

Spinoza's model of democracy was based on the provision of participation by virtue of civil status rather than by election. His notion of who had the right to participate in political life excluded women, servants, foreigners and those deemed not to have led respectable lives. Consequently, his model of democracy was limited to a relatively narrow section of society. However, unlike other elitist theorists of democracy, Spinoza tended to have a hopeful view of people's potential: he disagreed with the assertion that there is 'no truth or judgment in the common people', and believed that all 'men share in one and the same nature'[3]. As with the majority of future generations of liberal democrats, Spinoza regarded liberty as a first order principle and democracy as an instrument for its realisation. Spinoza, who wrote that 'the true aim of government is liberty', embraced democracy as medium through which this objective could be realised.

Whatever reservations Spinoza had about democracy were surpassed by his hostility towards monarchical and aristocratic forms of rule. One influential study of Spinoza's life contends that this philosopher's 'social feelings led him to sympathy with the common man; as a social scientist, however, he noted that common men were often irrational and hostile to freedom'[4]. Judging by his writings and behaviour, Spinoza comes across as a man divided between his democratic sympathies and his concern that people could be manipulated and misled by the anti-liberal Calvinist monarchist establishment in seventeenth-century Holland.

Spinoza was writing at the time of the establishment of the first republic in the Netherlands, and he was worried about the behaviour of what he saw as the 'superstitious Calvinist monarchist masses'. Along with his friend John de Witt, the head of the republic, Spinoza feared the capacity of the Calvinist establishment to stir up opposition to the new regime. During the course of writing his most important study, *Tractatus Theologico-Politicus* (*Theological-Political-Treatise*), Spinoza was preoccupied with questions such as:

Was the Republic then a form of government ahead of its time for the Netherlands? Could men of reason persuade the ordinary people that a republic would make for their greater happiness? Could men of reason undermine the irrational authority which benighted Calvinist divines exercised upon their congregations? How could the multitude be taught that freedom was their highest virtue?[5]

In the end, Spinoza's worst fears were realised when the Dutch lower classes turned against the republic and played an active role in its overthrow. The savage lynching of John de Witt had a profound impact on Spinoza's view of the world, and his apprehension mutated into a sense of bitterness about what he perceived as the irrationality of the masses. The man who once stated that 'in a free state, every man may think what he likes and say what he thinks' went on to argue that his *Theological-Political-Treatise* was not written for ordinary people because they were too prejudiced to give his ideas a hearing:

> To the rest of mankind I care not to commend my treatise; for I cannot expect that it contains anything to please them: I know how deeply are the prejudices embraced under the name of religion; I am aware that in the minds of the masses superstition is no less rooted than fear...they are led to praise or blame by impulse rather than reason[6].

Although it has been suggested that Spinoza penned these lines to get around the censor, it seems likely that this Plato-like view of the reader corresponded to his genuine feelings, as he appeared to become estranged from the democratic ideals that he championed. Even his belief in man's potential to play a public role became weaker, and instead of appealing to reason he opted for the politics of fear, writing that 'multitude becomes a thing to be feared if it has nothing to fear'[7]. The experience of history shows that the politics of fear renders people passive and undermines its potential for critically engaging with public life.

Spinoza was not able to resolve his contradictory attitude

towards democracy, remaining torn between his advocacy of a free society and his mistrust of the multitude. Unlike the other philosophers of his time, he was at least sympathetic to democracy, albeit in an anti-majoritarian form. What distinguished him from other anti-majoritarian commentators was that his outlook combined a strong anti-majoritarian attitude with a commitment to educate the masses to become more rational. In this sense, he provided encouragement to subsequent generations of thinkers, who would become drawn towards a more radical version of democracy.

Why the Enlightenment refused to take democracy seriously

The Enlightenment, which coincided with the Age of Reason, the Age of Revolutions and the Age of Democracy, possessed considerable potential for taking the role of popular consent seriously. The political and philosophical currents associated with the eighteenth-century Enlightenment believed that reason and science could be harnessed to the project of assisting humanity to assume greater control over its destiny. This movement asserted that reason shed the same light all over the world, that there was a single universal standard of justice, governed by one normative law, and that there was one human nature.

As the French philosopher Diderot explained, habits 'are not African or Asiatic or European. They are good or bad.' There are slaves 'under the Pole where it is very cold' and slaves 'in Constantinople where it is very hot'. Diderot wrote that 'everywhere a people should be educated, free and virtuous'[8]. Although Diderot was far more radical than most Enlightenment philosophers, they all attached great importance to the role that education could play to free the mind.

Diderot, like many of his colleagues, celebrated the power of reason and education, regarding this as the medium through which humans learned to improve their existence. Enlightenment thinkers refused to take the political norms and institutions that they inherited for granted. As the historian Jonathan Israel explains, the Enlightenment:

> ...not only attacked and severed the roots of traditional European culture in the sacred, magic, kingship, and hierarchy, secularising all institutions and ideas, but (intellectually and to a degree in practice) effectively demolished all legitimation of monarchy, aristocracy, woman's subordination to man, ecclesiastical authority, and slavery, replacing these with the principles of universality, equality and democracy[9].

Unfortunately, the principles of universality, equality and especially democracy were rarely acted upon, and were not actively promoted. The democratic potential of the Enlightenment was not realised because of the influence of intellectual and political currents suspicious of the people and the exercise of human agency. Like Spinoza, the leading figures of the Enlightenment stopped short of translating their commitment to human reason into a language of democratic solidarity.

It turned out that most Enlightenment thinkers were unclear about whether their new world included all people or a select few[10]. In the eighteenth century, leading Enlightenment figures were more likely to invest their hopes in a reforming legislator or ruler than in the intelligence of the people. Most philosophers, commentators and political economists assigned the gifted and morally superior Legislator or the Lawgiver the role of enlightening and educating the public, believing that the public could not be expected to develop its capacity to reason on its own. Though they acclaimed the power of human reasoning, they adopted a paternalistic attitude towards the question of putting trust in the average person's ability to reason.

Despite their criticism of the traditions and the customs of the past, Enlightenment thinkers tended to draw the conclusion that they could not quite do without their influence altogether. The main reason for their ambivalence was the premonition that if traditional institutions were dissolved, public disorder would ensue. That is why the late seventeenth-century French sceptic Pierre Bayle and the German philosopher Immanuel Kant opted for the enlightened rule of the absolute king. The eighteenth-century concept of 'enlightened despotism' indicated that for some, enlightenment depended far more on the contribution of an intelligent educated despot than on the intellectual resources of the people.

More than any other individual, Immanuel Kant has been identified as the embodiment of the Age of Reason that captured the imagination of educated Europeans in the eighteenth century. His motto 'Dare to Know' challenged his contemporaries to take charge of their lives and use their ability to reason to advance human development. 'Have the courage of your understanding,' he exhorted his audience,[11] claiming that enlightenment 'requires nothing but freedom'. Unfortunately, in his view, it did not require democracy. Kant opposed the rule of the majority, asserting that 'democracy is, properly speaking, necessarily despotism because it establishes an executive power in which "all" decide for or even against one who does not agree'[12]. According to his outlook, democracy contradicted freedom.

Like Spinoza, Kant found it difficult to reconcile freedom with democracy since he perceived majority rule as posing a threat to the liberty of the few. It is likely that Kant's fear of democracy, like that of his philosophical contemporaries, was a reaction to the political upheavals of his era. Popular outbursts of political frustration were interpreted by many leading supporters of the Enlightenment as a warning about reforming the old order too fast. For example, the outbreak of the Gordon Riots in London in 1780 reminded the elites of the threat posed by the urban masses, stalling the movement for reform in England and fostering a more hesitant attitude towards political change. The Gordon Riots moved the French economist and statesman Turgot to exclaim:

> To what stage [of civilization] has the human race advanced when in this century we see such fanaticism in London itself?[13]

It is important to underline the point that even the most radical sections of the Enlightenment drew back from embracing a whole-hearted embrace of democracy. Though they frequently declared their belief in the need to defend the interests of the people, they could not quite bring themselves to trust its capacity to reason and behave in a rational manner. Take Jean-Jacques Rousseau, the political philosopher usually associated with the radical wing of the Enlightenment. To this day, Rousseau is widely regarded as the most democratic of eighteenth-century Enlightenment philosophers – some go so far as to suggest that he was the *only* classical democratic theorist of his time. Yet despite his romantic view of human nature, he was profoundly pessimistic about the behaviour of real human beings and looked to a benevolent educator to give people direction.

Insofar as Rousseau possessed democratic impulses, they tended to be abstract and diffuse. He certainly did not believe in people's capacity to rule their society, believing that the job of governing could only be carried out responsibly by the select few. Rousseau outlined the important practical reasons why the people could not rule:

> If we take the term in the strict sense...there never has been a real democracy, and there never will be. It is against the natural order for the many to govern and the few to be governed. It is unimaginable that the people should remain continually assembled to devote their time to public affairs,

and it is clear that they cannot set up commissions for that purpose without the form of administration being changed[14].

For Rousseau, the obstacles to the realisation of people's rule were not only practical, but also to do with the moral qualities of the masses. That's why he concluded that 'were there a people of gods, their government would be democratic', adding: 'so perfect a government is not for men'.

The French revolutionary leader Maximilien Robespierre shared Rousseau's reservations, regarding individuals as powerless to resist the influence of prejudice and of social pressure. 'Human authority can always be attacked by human pride,' he claimed. Robespierre asserted that people lacked the capacity to reason and therefore they needed to be instructed by 'the religious sense by which the soul would be impressed with the idea of a sanction given to moral principles by a power superior to man'[15]. That a radical leader of the French Revolution embraced a 'power superior to man' illustrates the hesitant and selective manner with which the Age of Reason dealt with the relationship between individual liberty and authority. Optimistic beliefs about the capacity of education to set the individual free existed alongside the conviction that individuals in the here and now were likely to be 'wildly wrong'[16].

Despite its humanist aspirations the Enlightenment could not translate its ideals into a genuine affection or understanding of common people. Though many of the leading philosophers of the time quite rightly advocated the importance of education for improving society and mankind, they were prepared in practice to miseducate them – some even advocating the use of rituals, symbols and superstition, which they themselves did not believe in, to pacify the masses. As one commentator noted, Voltaire 'hates religious fanaticism; but he is certain that religion is necessary for the people if the rich are not to be murdered in their beds', adding that 'the God of Voltaire is a social necessity for the maintenance of order; without him there would be no restraint upon the behaviour of men'[17]. The corollary of Voltaire's cynical use of religion was the view that there was little point in trying to reason with an uneducated mass who can only respond to irrational appeals to the emotions.

Despite the intensely polarised political climate of the late-eighteenth century, both supporters and opponents of the French Revolution agreed on the point that some kind of religion was required to guide public conduct. Mistrust of the people transcended the divide between pro and anti-Enlightenment commentators, as both sides sought to manipulate religion as an instrument for gaining people's acquiescence to order and stability.

That the Enlightenment lost its nerve when confronted with the issue of popular democracy is beyond doubt. This loss of nerve is particularly striking in Kant's case, as he went to great lengths to explain why paternalistic government constituted the 'worst possible despotism one can imagine'. He rightly noted that in such circumstances, people are relegated to the role of minors 'who cannot distinguish between what is good and what is bad for them' and are therefore 'forced to adopt a passive role'[18]. Yet despite his astute critique of paternalist rule, Kant still opted to reject the one form of *political* rule that is most committed to challenging the passive behaviour of citizens.

A legacy of suspicion

As I discuss in the next chapter, despite the attempt to keep democracy at bay, in the nineteenth century the demand of the many for more political rights could not be contained. The French Revolution anticipated the development of mass politics. In contrast to previous plebeian movements, the urban masses of the nineteenth century voiced their demands in a coherent egalitarian and democratic form. In Europe, the masses would prove to be a formidable force, one that regularly called into question the legitimacy of the prevailing political arrangements.

Although suspicion continued to pervade the discussion around the political role of the people, the nineteenth century saw the steady extension of the franchise. A begrudging acceptance of representative democracy coexisted with the legacy of mistrust, and this uneasy relationship persisted well into the twentieth century. From the 1870s onwards, conservative and liberal thinkers expressed serious doubts about the capacity of the multitude to play the role of responsible citizens, and from the 1920s onwards, a loss of faith in the moral integrity of the multitude also characterised the mood of a significant section of the radical left.

The German radical psychologist and philosopher Erich Fromm thus combined his critique of capitalist culture with a pessimistic diagnosis of 1930s public life:

> We have been compelled to recognize that millions in Germany were as eager to surrender their freedom as their fathers were to fight for it[19].

John Dewey, the leading theorist of the American progressive movement, regarded the psychological attitudes of the masses as a threat to democracy in the United States. 'The serious threat to our democracy,' he asserted, 'is not the existence of foreign totalitarian states' but the 'existence within our personal attitudes and within our own institutions of conditions which have given a victory to external authority, discipline, uniformity and dependence upon The Leader'[20].

Since the turn of the twenty-first century the traditional fear of the people has acquired the form of a veritable *demophobia*. The main expression of demophobia is its unrestrained hatred of populism. Paradoxically, critics of populist movements accuse it of practising the politics of fear. But in reality, it is the fear of populism that offers the most systematic expression of the politics of fear. That is why invariably critics of populism conclude their alarmist accounts with the warning that unless they are crushed, populism will lead to the rise of another Hitler.

Chapter 5

Taming democracy

Following the upheavals of the eighteenth century, it was impossible to turn back the clock and ignore the demand of a growing section of the people for political rights and a greater voice. Although sections of the European elites were devoted to keeping democracy at bay, there was a growing realisation among the new industrial and middle classes that concessions had to be made to demands for political reform. The rising middle class resented the privileges associated with the aristocracy, and rejected the traditional arguments about the sanctity of the traditional hierarchy. In any case, the aspirations of the newly-formed urban middle classes were inconsistent with a hierarchy based on birth. Many of them sought to consolidate their status through claiming moral and intellectual leadership over the popular movements that emerged towards the last quarter of the eighteenth century. Political reform provided opportunities for the expression of democratic ideals.

The late-eighteenth and early-nineteenth centuries saw the appearance of genuine radical democratic voices, such as Thomas Paine and leaders of the British Chartist Movement, who put forward powerful arguments about the virtues of a democratic republic. Paine argued that a true republic is one where democracy is based on the principles of equality and consent and where citizens decide for themselves the direction of their society. His pamphlet *The Age of Reason* (1776) and other publications communicated a passionate defence of liberal democracy[1]. To this day, the power and coherence of his argument for the necessity of democratic consent and liberty remains unmatched. *The Age of Reason* became an instant bestseller and more than 100,000 copies circulated among the two million residents of the 13 colonies in North America. The response to Paine's publications on both sides of the Atlantic indicated that there was a real demand by the reading public for radical democratic ideas.

The growth of radicalism, which was aided by the proliferation of new publications, helped fuel the development of mass politics and the expansion of public life. Writing in 1830, the liberal philosopher James Mill described this new political landscape in the following terms:

> The Art of printing exists. And the irresistible progress of the information which it diffuses necessitates, not a change merely, but a perfect revolution in the art of governing mankind. In the times that are gone, the art of government has consisted in a mixture of fraud and force in which, commonly, the fraud predominated. In the times that are to come, as fraud will be impracticable, and as knowledge of what is good and what is evil in the mode of managing the national affairs cannot be withheld from the nation, government will be left either to rational conviction, or to naked force. This is the grand revolution of modern times[2].

Mill's 'grand revolution of modern times' did not refer merely to the diffusion of knowledge, but also to the transformation of public life in a modern urbanised and industrial world. The question facing James Mill and the middle-class elite was how to manage the demand of a new assertive and articulate public for a greater political voice.

The challenge posed by demands for political reform forced their opponents to develop persuasive arguments against calls for democratic advance. Anti-democratic arguments and theories were re-configurated to meet the challenge posed by the popular movements demanding political reform in the nineteenth century.

The old arguments about the tyranny of the majority and the dangers posed by violent mobs did not disappear. However, increasingly, anti-democratic sentiments tended to be promoted through more subtle and indirect forms. One of the ways in which the problem of the *demos* was reframed was through the concept of public opinion. Public opinion often served as a code through which concerns about the maintenance of law and order were communicated. For commentators associated with the rising middle class in the nineteenth century, the concept of public opinion provided a narrative through which the management of the relationship between the educated elites and the lower classes could be discussed.

At the time, public opinion was frequently referred to as a powerful force. Some commentators contended that public opinion was omnipotent, and that therefore even monarchs and secular rulers had no choice but to yield to its influence. As the Liberal politician James Bryce reminded his readers, it was 'only by rare exception that a monarch or an oligarchy has maintained authority against the will of the people'.

However, discussions of public opinion were characteristically vague about what its power meant. They also left open the crucial questions of who represented public opinion, whose opinions counted, and whose views need not be taken seriously. Ultimately, the most important problem facing the educated elites was to gain authority over public opinion. At least in the early part of the nineteenth century, representatives of the educated liberal middle class were hopeful that the people would defer to their knowledge and wisdom and that therefore they could guide public opinion. This sentiment was forcefully expressed by James Mill in 1820:

> The opinions of that class of the people, who are below the middle rank, are formed, and their minds directed by that intelligent and virtuous rank, who come most immediately in

contact with them, to whom they fly for advice and assistance in all their numerous difficulties, upon whom they feel an immediate and daily dependence, in health and in sickness, in infancy, and in old age: to whom their children look up as models for their imitation, whose opinion they hear daily repeated, and account it their honour to adopt[3].

No doubt this was a statement of wishful thinking, and in the decades to follow, public opinion often refused to defer to the views of the educated elites.

The educated elites continually attempted to establish themselves as an authority that could decide what counted as legitimate public opinion. Not surprisingly, they tended to equate their view of the world with the opinion of the public. This attitude was most coherently articulated by the voices of the nineteenth-century liberal elites, whose support for expanding the electoral franchise was contingent on their ability to represent public opinion. Many British liberal reformers and utilitarian philosophers, such as Jeremy Bentham, presumed that they could serve as the authoritative voice of public opinion. As one study points out, the support of Bentham and his group for political democracy was linked to the claim that 'the public to be trusted was the English middle class', which they viewed 'as the most rational political class that had ever appeared in history'[4].

At the outset of the nineteenth century, liberal and utilitarian thinkers were reasonably optimistic about their capacity to harness the authority of public opinion to support their wider objectives. But by the 1850s, optimism gave way to apprehensions about public opinion's unpredictable and potentially threatening trajectory. Such sentiments were a sublimated expression of elite concerns about how to manage the growth of democratic aspirations and the enfranchisement of the majority. As we shall see, the narrative of public opinion expressed its ambivalence towards democracy through a critique of mass politics. At times, this ambivalence turned into fear that the masses would ignore the wise counsel of their social superiors and embrace radical democratic sentiments.

Taming public opinion

From the late-eighteenth century onwards, voices representing the newly emergent bourgeoisie sought to tame public opinion by defining it as an expression of its outlook. They typically asserted that only certain types of people were 'capable' of expressing public opinion, while the rest were 'seen as being in particular need of its (supposedly wholesome) influence'[5]. The French philosopher Condorcet distinguished between *public* opinion and *popular* opinion, stating that 'whereas public opinion is enlightened by the men of letters, popular opinion is that of "the most stupid and most misery-stricken part of the people"'[6]. Condorcet's contempt for popular opinion typified the elitist premise that underpinned the conceptualisation of public opinion, and it is worth pointing out that his views on this question influenced the thinking of the founding fathers of the United States.

Following Condorcet's approach, in the UK, William MacKinnon's 1828 pioneering study of public opinion made a distinction between the opinion of the educated public and that of the rest of society, by contrasting the 'public opinion' of the educated with the 'public clamour' of the multitude[7]. For MacKinnon, 'public clamour' was the articulation of sentiments that he did not like, such as populist or radical views. MacKinnon associated public opinion with the educated and refined sentiments of the middle class and public clamour with the ignorant displays of emotion of 'excitement created amongst the uneducated, or amongst those who do not reflect, or do not exercise their judgement on the point in question'[8].

Liberal and conservative contributions on the subject implicitly echoed the unfavourable comparison drawn between the opinions of the educated and the uneducated. George Cornwall Lewis, in *An Essay on the Influence of Authority in Matters of Opinion* (1849), self-consciously drew a contrast between the 'small number of competent judges on each subject – the guides to opinion who constitute authority' and 'the large majority who are uninformed and inexperienced in the matter, and unfit to guide others by their judgement[9]'.

Lewis regarded the expansion of the franchise as a necessary evil for endowing governing with legitimacy. His view on democracy was influenced by an aristocratic liberal suspicion of the rule of the majority, and he claimed that 'the secret of a free constitution' was the capacity of the 'principle of special fitness' to counteract the influence of the morally inferior 'numerical principal'[10]. As with numerous commentators on the subject, Lewis believed that the taming of the opinion of the many required that the intellectual authority of the elites over them was widely recognised.

The radical liberal philosopher J.S. Mill also based his arguments for democratic representative government on the assumption that there was a difference in the knowledge and opinion of the 'few' and that of the 'many'. He stated that for 'the formation of the best public opinion, there should exist somewhere a great social support for opinions and sentiments different from those of the mass'[11]. What counted for Mill were those sentiments that he believed the masses did not and, most likely, could not, possess. He believed that political democracy depended on the deference of the masses to the 'best public opinion'.

J.S. Mill supposed that the power of persuasion was the most effective way of avoiding instability and conflict, writing that the 'only hope from class legislation in its narrowest, and political ignorance in its most dangerous form would lie in such disposition as the uneducated might have to choose educated representatives and defer to their opinion'[12]. In other words: if the uneducated understood that their interests could be best enforced if they deferred to the opinions of their educated superiors, political stability could be maintained.

Mill's argument for deference was founded in a belief in the authority of the knowledge of the expert. Although he was inclined to be more democratic than most of his liberal contemporaries, he allocated a central role for elected expert representatives in the drafting of legislation, insisting that it was 'so important that the electors should choose as their representatives wiser men than themselves, and should consent to be governed according to that superior wisdom'[13].

That Mill, arguably the most radical liberal philosopher of the nineteenth century and an eloquent defender of freedom and liberty, had such a low opinion of the uneducated masses highlights the fear of democracy that dominated the imagination of the nineteenth-century political establishment. Mill was far more sympathetic to the lower classes than his fellow liberals, but he was also an unapologetic advocate of the idea of a 'clerisy', an endowed class whose apparent wisdom and intelligence entitled them to possess the authority to guide the lives of the average person.

For utilitarian and liberal thinkers, deference meant that the opinion of the intellectual and scientific community should be upheld as authoritative by society. Reconciling the principle of majority rule with deference would constitute one of the central problems of modern liberalism. The nineteenth-century European political class recognised that sooner or later it would have to give way to the popular pressure for democratic reform. The French socialist Saint-Simon who constructed an elaborate theory justifying social hierarchy, nevertheless recognised that a bargain had to be struck with the 'claims of equality' because 'no order could be maintained except on a mass basis'[14].

Pragmatism toward the management of public opinion ran in parallel with the recognition that it was a potentially dangerous force that had to be contained. The growth of trade unions and radical movements in the nineteenth century highlighted the threat posed by popular movements that freed themselves from the political influence of the educated elites. In response, the tone of the discussion became increasingly defensive and pessimistic, as numerous commentators recycled the classical anti-democratic pathologies of the multitude – ignorance, susceptible to corruption, envious of other's status and wealth – and coupled public opinion with the peril posed by the tyranny of the majority.

The great fear

In the nineteenth century, the indirect attacks on democracy were infused with a variety of contradictory sentiments, ranging from false confidence, scepticism and contempt towards the people to outright fear of the tyranny of the majority. A half-hearted acquiescence to the expansion of the franchise coexisted with a determination to do what was necessary to limit the political influence of the lower classes. As Hamilton explains:

> Classical liberals in the early decades of the nineteenth century had profound forebodings concerning the apparently inevitable advent of democracy. In response, they advocated elitism as a brake on the 'tyranny of the majority'[15].

Hamilton argues that these sentiments have endured, and that 'elitism today is the residue of the liberal scepticism concerning democratic government'[16].

From the 1830s onwards, assessments of public opinion became increasingly defensive and pessimistic. For example, Mill became concerned about what would happen if general opinion was not influenced by 'enlightened doctrines propounded by more cultivated minds'. His focus was now on the question of how the influence of the educated clerisy could shape and direct public opinion, and his concern regarding the tyranny of the majority was compounded by his suspicion that 'even wise men are capable of being corrupted'[17]. Despite his liberal enthusiasm for freedom and individual autonomy, Mill had a low opinion of the people, suggesting that, 'it is not for the people to govern, but only to choose a well-qualified assembly to govern for them'[18].

Mill's attitude was influenced by Alexis de Tocqueville's analysis of public opinion in the United States. Tocqueville's *Democracy in America* serves as one of the most influential versions of an indirect attack on, and critique of, democracy. Tocqueville treated democracy and public opinion as a regrettable fact of life that inevitably led to the deterioration of the quality of culture and threatened individual and minority interests. He used his study of American democracy as a warning of the threat posed by Europe's accommodation to pressure for majority rule.

Tocqueville portrayed majoritarian politics as a malevolent force that enforced the conformity of all to popular opinion. He warned how, in the United States, 'the power of the majority surpasses all the powers with which we are acquainted in Europe', writing that once the majority has made a decision 'everyone is silent, and the friends as well as the opponents of the measure unite in assenting to its propriety'. Tocqueville claimed that the power of the majority is far greater than that of an absolutist monarch, since 'no monarch is so absolute as to combine all the powers of society in his own hands and to conquer all opposition, as a majority is able to do, which has the right both of making and of executing the laws'[19].

Tocqueville's dramatic rendition of the all-pervasive power of opinion makes an authoritarian tyrant appear relatively impotent. In Tocqueville's imagination, whereas 'the authority of a king is physical and controls the actions of men without subduing their will', public opinion can overwhelm the internal life of people. Tocqueville argued that the authority of public opinion was so formidable that a 'man who raises his voice in the cause of truth' has less protection in the United States than he would even in an absolutist state[20].

Tocqueville's warnings about the power of public opinion in America captured the European elite's unease with the growing influence of the 'many' and the uncertain and contingent status of its own authority. While Tocqueville may have been more hostile to this power than those of more liberal or radical inclinations, the sense of omnipotence he attributed to it was integral to the conventional wisdom of the era. Not for nothing was public opinion anointed as the new religion of industrial Europe. The German historian Barthold Georg Niebuhr expressed this sentiment when he declared:

> Public opinion is that opinion which in spite of the difference in individuals and of the very different conditions or situations in which they are placed, is so unanimously expressed, and merely represented by one man after another, that it may be taken as the utterance of universal truth and reason, and even as the will of God itself[21].

Niebuhr's representation of public opinion as a modern equivalent of an utterance of divine will resonated with the temper of the times.

By the end of the nineteenth century, public opinion was regularly portrayed as a threat to social order and civilisation. It was depicted as a 'power and influence' that literally forced politicians and statesmen to act against their better judgement. Often this destructive influence was blamed on the press, which both gave voice to and shaped this force. As a result, wrote a commentator in the conservatively-inclined *National Review*, 'leading statesmen grow more and more into opportunists, and are more and more compelled to say, not what they themselves think ought to be said, but what, in their judgment, the audience they address would like to have said'[22]. This sentiment was widely shared by writers who increasingly depicted public opinion as a medium through which a new form of tyranny could subjugate everyone to conform to the base tastes and customs of the lower orders. Towards the end of the century, E.A. Ross, one of the leading lights of the American progressive movement, warned that the 'wholesome sway of public opinion may degenerate into a fierce tyranny of the multitude, making for conformity, conservatism, and stagnation'[23].

Pessimistic accounts of public opinion were based on the realisation that liberal and conservative political elites alike were losing influence over the urban masses. As one study pointed out, public opinion 'as the expression of the middle class, with its classical liberalism, failed to retain the loyalty of the masses of men'[24]. Expectation that public opinion could be managed now gave way to the fear that it was an inherently unstable and therefore unpredictable force which not only legitimated authority, but also threatened it. Yet as an indirect expression of the democratisation of public life, it was a phenomenon that could not be ignored. With the passing of time, commentaries on public opinion were increasingly and instinctively drawn towards the project of seeking to delegitimate its influence.

Anxiety about maintaining elite influence over the people endures to this day and constitutes the main driver of the vilification of populism. Democracy Panic regarding the loss of elite influence over the behaviour and attitude of the people is frequently expressed in the anti-populist narrative. It claims that public life in the twenty-first century is 'swiftly erasing almost any elite moderation or control of our democratic discourse'[25]. This statement, which echoes the concerns raised by Mill and De Tocqueville almost 2 centuries ago, speaks to the durability of the project of taming public opinion. Since the public could never be entirely tamed, the goal of retaining the hegemony of elite influence has turned into a never-ending quest.

As we discuss in Chapter 7, one of the strategies adopted to de-legitimate public opinion and, by implication, democracy was to call into question the psychological state of the people. The new discipline of psychology was used to cast doubt on the mental state of the people and to divest public opinion from association with any positive attributes. The other important component of the war against public opinion was to blame mass culture and the media for the dangerous and unpredictable influence of public opinion: an attack used to deflect attention from the failure of the middle class to retain its influence.

Blaming the corrosive impact of mass culture and, especially, the media became one of the most effective arguments used against democracy. It succeeded in calling into question the ability of the many to play the role of responsible citizens. To this day, blaming the media and mass culture is practised by both the Left and the Right. The next chapter examines how attacks on mass culture and so-called 'mass man' became one of the key themes promoted in the silent war against democracy.

Chapter 6

Mass culture

Since the nineteenth century, two of the key targets of critics of democracy have been *mass culture* and *mass society*. Critics of mass society claim that its main distinguishing features are conformist, morally dissolute and irrational behaviour. But their main concern is the modern imperative towards equality and democracy, which they indict for the disorganisation of social life. Democracy is not attacked directly here – rather, critics focus their fire on the influence of egalitarian and democratic trends upon the creation of a diseased and debased mass culture.

The moral condemnation of mass culture often serves as a roundabout way of highlighting people's alleged conformity and gullibility. According to this view, mass society produces a type of 'mass man' who, lacking the habit of independence, desperately seeks to conform to the prevailing sentiments. Deficient in judgement and the ability to understand the issues of the day, mass man is said to be easily manipulated by unscrupulous politicians, advertisers and the media.

Though the invective is directed at mass culture and the media, the conclusion that is invariably drawn is that the problem is the people, who are all too ready to become spiritually and mentally enslaved by demagogues and psychological manipulators. This kind of polemic outwardly condemns the power of the media over an easily misled audience, but its main target is the feeble moral status of an electorate that cannot discriminate between truth and fiction. Of course, there are legitimate criticisms to be made of mass culture and the media. But the main driver of anti-mass ideology is not concern with the quality of culture, but the project of diseasing its audience.

Over the past century, anti-mass culture ideology has proven to be one of the most enduring and powerful weapons in the armoury of anti-democratic forces. Attacks on the power of mass culture and the media have found support across the conventional political divide. Typically, sections of the Right criticise mass culture for encouraging the selfish, violent behaviour of the people, whereas the Left regards them as the hapless and easily manipulated victims of an omnipotent mass media.

The earliest formulation of this thesis of mass culture can be found in the writings of the conservative critic of the French Revolution, Joseph de Maistre. He feared the power of the passions of the masses and regarded the influence of democratic and egalitarian sentiments as a threat to European civilisation. De Maistre warned that, 'if the crowd who are governed can believe they are the equal of the small number who actually govern, *government no longer exists*'[1]. He made no attempt to disguise his hatred for democracy; his animosity was fuelled by the belief that the 'crowd' was composed of essentially primitive and unintelligent people who were incapable of exercising self-restraint or reason.

The tendency to view the masses as if they were a different race to the refined members of the educated middle classes was by no means confined to hard-core conservative writers. Many radical liberals and socialists, who were disappointed by the refusal of the people to embrace their enlightened views, made little attempt to disguise their revulsion. The English socialist and social psychologist Graham Wallas expressed his disappointment with mass democracy through a language that matched de Maistre's tone. His description of working-class women being mobilised to vote by a canvasser during a London County Council election at the turn of the twentieth century conveys a tone of barely concealed contempt:

About half of them were women, with broken straw hats, pallid faces, and untidy hair. All were dazed and bewildered, having been snatched away in carriages and motors from the making of match-boxes, button holes, or cheap furniture, or from the public house, or, since it was Saturday evening, from bed[2].

Wallas' patronising description of the voting behaviour of working-class women in London corresponded to the views of the emerging all-party anti-mass consensus. In the interwar era, this sentiment was most lucidly developed by the Spanish philosopher José Ortega y Gasset, in his influential book, *The Revolt of The Masses*. Ortega y Gasset asserted that the 'mass crushes beneath it everything that is different, everything that is excellent, individual, qualified, and select'. He highlighted a theme that frequently recurs in the silent war against democracy, which holds that the mass man cannot think for himself, is instinctively conformist and dislikes those who aspire to be different and those who question majority opinion. Ortega y Gasset went so far as to warn that 'anybody who is not like everybody, who does not think like everybody, runs the risk of being eliminated'[3].

In the 1930s, the concerns raised by Ortega y Gasset were shared – albeit from a radically different standpoint – by leading thinkers associated with the Marxisant Frankfurt School, such as Herbert Marcuse, Theodore Adorno and Max Horkheimer. They criticised mass culture on the grounds that it deprived people of the capacity for critical thought. Although they saw themselves as radical critics of capitalism, they could not quite bring themselves to trust the people. Herbert Marcuse, one of the heroes of the 1960s New Left, regarded people as the passive victims of American consumer culture, arguing that the hypnotic power of the mass media indoctrinated and conditioned people to the point that they became passive objects of its manipulation[4].

Whereas in the early part of the twentieth century, elite theories of mass society tended to be authored by conservative and right-wing ideologues, in the post-Second World War era, they were more likely to express the disappointment of liberal and left-wing commentators. In 1950, Adorno, arguably one of the most important academic cultural theorists of the era, baldly stated that the people were captivated by propaganda and psychological manipulation. He warned about the 'spell of a thought-controlling mass culture' which 'has become almost universal'[5]. Referring back to ancient Greece he echoed Plato's view that, 'the majority of the people frequently act blindly in accordance with the will of powerful institutions or demagogic figures'[6].

In recent times, the tendency to view people as the hapless victims of the mass media has become even more widespread among contemporary leftist critics of mass culture. Commentators sometimes go so far as to hold the mass media guilty of turning its audience into brainwashed subjects. In 2016, the American filmmaker Jen Senko made a film of her father, who she believes was indoctrinated into fear by the conservative media. 'All of these emotions, especially fear, whip people up into a state of alarm,' stated Senko, before asserting that it is 'like a disease infecting millions of people around the country'[7].

Senko might be surprised to discover that her critique of the 'conservative media' shares the premise on which most anti-democratic theories are founded. The view that people lack the critical faculties to think reasonably, and to make choices that are in their interests and those of their community, is the foundation on which most anti-democratic sentiments are founded. The difference between a reactionary like de Maistre and Senko is this: de Maistre actively despises democracy, while Senko merely wants democracy without a *demos*.

Suspicion of the media, and mistrust of the people

Throughout history, the media has been the focus of constant anxiety – and this is not surprising. Even before the emergence of the mass media, concerns were raised about its destabilising influence on the people. Since the discovery of writing, political and religious rulers have worried about their ability to control information and ideas; as we have seen, Plato actively promoted censorship because he feared the consequences of the dissemination of the written text. Similar sentiments were expressed by leading theologians and philosophers during the centuries to follow.

It was not until the eighteenth-century Enlightenment that elite views about the influence of reading became more relaxed. The Enlightenment fostered a climate that encouraged education, with some commentators even regarding reading as a medium through which society could be reformed. Yet even then, there were conflicting interpretations about whether the new mass readership constituted a force for good or evil.

Almost all the leading philosophers and commentators had contradictory attitudes towards the reader. They invariably acclaimed those who read to study or to improve themselves, while decrying unruly or indiscriminate reading practices. Despite their advocacy of moral autonomy, many Enlightenment thinkers took for granted that the reading public lacked the ability to discriminate between truth and falsehood and feared that the availability of cheaply-produced popular fiction would estrange people from the fine words of their educated superiors.

Their objection was not to reading as such, but to the reading of material that distracted people from appreciating the promise of the Enlightenment. In the late-eighteenth and early-nineteenth centuries, such distractions were often medicalised in the language of addiction, which was targeted at the novel. It was alleged that tales of romance and adventure provided no benefit to the reader; indeed, they encouraged people to read 'excessively'. Reading 'for its own sake' was presented as not only a purposeless but also a potentially corrupting activity.

The eighteenth-century narrative associating reading with the pathology of addiction communicated three recurring themes. The first is a lack of confidence in the capacity of elite culture to influence and direct the reading taste of the wider public. The second is contempt towards popular tastes, which expresses itself with the certainty that the public will be drawn to the most debased and corrupting literary influences. The third inflates the power of the written word to control human behaviour, with members of the public presented as literally helpless to resist the manipulative influence of that written word. Against such an omnipotent and irresistible force, it was argued, the worthy literature of Enlighteners simply could not compete.

These three themes influence discussions of mass culture to this day. If anything, the current dominant discourse about media power, internet addiction and fake news is even more sceptical about people's ability to resist the corrupting influence of mass culture.

In the nineteenth century, the current tendency to view the media as an omnipotent force gained traction. General unease with the uncertain direction of a changing world was expressed through a language of suspicion and foreboding about the influence of the press and popular literature. These anxieties intensified with the growing commercialisation of publishing and the availability of cheaply-produced texts.

The discussion of mass culture in the nineteenth century reflected the ambiguity of the ruling elites towards the democratisation of reading. At times, sections of the Establishment who understood the need to extend political reform hoped that reading and education would encourage the lower orders to adopt the world view of the middle classes. They rightly understood that there was a connection between the expansion of a reading public and the democratisation of cultural life but became disappointed when it turned out that the readers of the mass media adopted opinions and behaviours that contradicted the expectations of middle-class reformers. From this point onwards, expressions of scepticism towards mass culture and mass man serve as a marker for communicating disappointment about the working of democracy.

There was, and continues to be, a significant element of hypocrisy in the way that mass culture is portrayed. If indeed there were genuine concerns with the cultural deficits of the masses, the obvious solution was the encouragement of education, reading and other intellectual pursuits. But instead, critics of mass culture opted to restrain the public's appetite for reading and other forms of media consumption.

Liberalism's uneasy relationship with mass society

Despite its positive reforming impulses, classical liberalism always possessed an elitist dimension. Its elitist sensibility was often expressed through a quasi-aristocratic disdain for what it perceived as the corrupting influence of mass culture and society. Even relatively radical liberals tended to portray the lower classes as an unreliable mass that could be easily corrupted or led astray by unscrupulous demagogues.

In 1919, the English political theorist Harold Laski warned that 'few things have been more easy than for an able and energetic government, which was willing to pay the price, to bribe a whole people into slavery'[8]. Laski, who became the chairman of the British Labour Party in 1945, personified the paternalistic disdain with which the socialist establishment viewed 'a whole people'.

The interwar years saw the transformation of the nineteenth-century mass culture narrative into a modern version of the ancient anti-democratic argument about the incapacity of the multitude to act as responsible citizens. These new arguments offered an exaggerated account of the dominance of mass culture, particularly with regard to the media and the new technologies of propaganda. Looking back on extravagant claims made about the power of the media and mass propaganda, it is possible to conclude that they provided liberal politicians and thinkers with an alibi that justified their failure to influence the masses.

During the decades following the First World War, liberal thinkers more or less gave up on the possibility of influencing the masses. Their account of mass society and the irrationality of its people often comes across as an apology for their failure to compete with movements of the radical Left and the Right. If the masses were as fickle and as easily seduced by the propaganda of the mass media as they were said to be, liberalism could blame its failures on circumstances beyond its control. According to this simplistic account, the rise of fascism and communism was a consequence of propaganda and manipulation. The difficulty that liberal and conservative political leaders had in challenging the ideological appeal of their radical foes was often blamed on skilful demagogues.

John Dewey, one of the most important American liberal thinkers of the twentieth century, sought to account for the crisis of his creed by offering an analysis that suggested that mass society was inhospitable to the workings of a rational democracy. Although Dewey avoided adopting the explicit contempt that the elite theories of his time directed towards the masses, he still characterised the emotional life of the American public as 'undiscriminating, lacking in individuality and in direction by intellectual life'. His diagnosis of the problem was that 'our pronounced trait is mass suggestibility'[9].

The concept of mass suggestibility served as a moral condemnation of both mass culture and the mass man, who was defined by his gullibility. For the British sociologist Morris Ginsberg, 'the political ignorance of the masses and their gullibility' was constantly reinforced by 'the existence of highly developed machinery for steady and cumulative suggestion'[10]. Writing in 1921, Ginsberg painted a frightening picture of the power of advertising and propaganda:

Advertising and propaganda generally deliberately make their appeal to powerful emotional tendencies and instincts, the arousal of which tends to inhibit conflicting ideas and therefore reduce the powers of criticism to a low level. Further, by dint of steady repetition, they have an enormous cumulative effect, moulding the opinions and sentiments of their publics and, what is perhaps more dangerous, subtly creating in their victims the illusion that they are really thinking for themselves instead of receiving their opinions ready made[11].

If the public was so susceptible to manipulation that they not only passively absorbed its manipulator's opinions but also believed that they were 'really thinking of themselves', there was very little hope that democracy could work. In such circumstances the electorate was reduced to the role of a passive audience, whose views were not the outcome of rational debate but what we would today call 'fake news'.

In the 1920s and 1930s, pessimistic accounts of the influence of mass propaganda and culture coincided with a loss of faith in political reform and democracy. Old questions about the reliability of democratic citizenship were re-raised through the discussion of mass culture and mass man. Public opinion, which was always a focus of anxiety, came under new attack and was routinely depicted as a synthesis of irrational myths and prejudice. This argument was forcefully presented by the American commentator Walter Lippmann in his influential 1992 study *Public Opinion*, which declared that the proportion of the electorate that is 'absolutely illiterate' is much larger than one would suspect, and that these people who are 'mentally children or barbarians' are the natural targets of manipulators.

The belief that the public was dominated by infantile emotions was widely echoed by opinion makers in the interwar period, often conveying the assumption that public opinion does not know what is in its best interests.

The scepticism expressed by a leading American political scientist, Harold Lasswell, characterised his discipline's attitude towards democratic public life. He denounced people with democratic inclinations for 'deceiving themselves' and claimed that the power of propaganda to manipulate the masses called into question 'the traditional species of democratic romanticism'[12].

Disappointment with democratic politics was reflected through an intensified tendency to discredit public opinion. As one important study of this trend points out:

> The experience of the [First] World War intensified the tendency to emphasize the non-rational forces involved in the formation or manipulation of public opinion, and it promoted a deep and wide-spread scepticism as to the validity of democratic theory in general and the competence of public opinion in particular[13].

By the mid-1930s, democracy itself was held responsible for unleashing the destructive and irrational powers sweeping the world. In his 1933 essay 'The Democratization of Culture', the sociologist Karl Mannheim asserted that it was democracy that created the terrain for the flourishing of totalitarian movements:

> Dictatorships can arise only in democracies; they are made possible by the greater fluidity introduced into political life by democracy. Dictatorship is not the antithesis of democracy; it represents one of the possible ways in which a democratic society may try to solve its problems[14].

Mannheim regarded the gullibility of the masses to be an 'aspect of the irrational thirst of the modern populace for "wish fulfilment"', which led to the acceptance of the political fantasies of a totalitarian age[15]. His negative account of mass democracy was elaborated through a dystopian vision of mass society and mass men:

> In a society in which the masses tend to dominate, irrationalities which have not been integrated into the social structure may force their way into political life. This situation is dangerous because the selective apparatus of mass democracy opens the door to irrationalities in those places where rational direction is indispensable. Thus, democracy itself produces its own antithesis and even provides its enemies with their weapons[16].

Mannheim's pessimism towards the working of mass democracy reflected views that were widely held by the Anglo-American political establishment in the 1930s and 1940s. Since the time of ancient Athens, democracy has been depicted as the terrain on which tyranny breeds: and theories of mass society developed this theme further, by indicting democracy for creating the conditions for fascism to flourish. The erroneous view that a misled electorate voted Adolf Hitler into power continues to influence anti-populist views to this day.

The legacy of mass man

Historically, the conceptualisation of mass man was mainly associated with a conservative elitist imagination; and sections of the conservative intelligentsia continue to hold on to a negative view of mass democratic culture. Following Ortega, the Polish conservative philosopher Ryszard Legutko writes of the 'aridity of the democratic mind'. He contends that democracy has 'an ability to change the whole mindset of society by depriving it of all intellectual and psychological impulses, all social habits and aspirations, however creative and valuable, that did not conform to democratic practices'.

Legutko's concern is 'the danger of mediocrity' that democratic rule imposes on modern society[17]. His association of democracy and the 'increasing role of the masses' with the 'vulgarisation of culture' constitutes an important theme in the classical conservative critique of mass society.

On the other side, so-called Cultural Marxists often hold popular and consumer culture in contempt, and their elitist disdain for the vulgarisation of culture often matches the tone of conservative critics. From the 1920s onwards, a loss of faith in the moral integrity of the multitude began to influence a significant section of the Left.

In the aftermath of the Second World War, anti-mass ideology retained its influence. An influential leftist version of this ideology was provided by Adorno and other social scientists associated with the Frankfurt School, who developed a paternalistic view of the masses as needing protection from their own irrational behaviour. Adorno asserted that it was 'naively idealistic' to imagine that a 'thought-controlling mass culture' could be fought 'through intellectual means alone'. Instead, he called for relying on counter-propaganda to help people realise what their real interest really is.

Adorno's reliance on top-down propaganda to counter the influence of authoritarian ideologies indicated a profound sense of estrangement from the tradition of democratic discussion and debate. He wrote that anti-authoritarian leadership must make the people 'conscious of their own wants and needs as against ideologies which are hammered into their heads by the innumerable communications of vested interests'[18]. That's another way of saying that the people needed Adorno and his colleagues to tell them what was in their best interests.

Adorno's assertion that since people are not aware of their true interests, they need the help of enlightened leaders to guide their political choices is widely echoed by anti-populist commentators in the contemporary era. 'People getting their fundamental interests wrong is what American political life is all about,' notes Thomas Frank in the US bestseller *What's the Matter*

With Kansas? Otherwise, he asks, how could they possibly vote for the Republicans? Similar explanations were used to explain why people voted for Donald Trump and Brexit.

Time and again, the power of mass culture over mass man has served as a warning against the working of democracy. The power of demagogues, propaganda or the media over society has served as an explanation of the irrational attributes of public opinion. Although attacks on mass culture and the media often assume a radical form, they convey a deeply pessimistic view of the democratic potential of ordinary people.

The moral condemnation of mass man serves to call into question the ability of most people to play the role of a responsible citizen. If indeed people are unable to think for themselves and offer themselves up as puppets to be manipulated by tabloid journals and the media, there is little hope for democracy. And if mass culture is omnipotent, then with the exception of a chosen few, just about everyone becomes mentally enslaved by forces beyond their control, and democracy turns into a fantasy.

Criticism of mass culture has provided a get-out clause for politicians and ideologues who find it difficult to take responsibility for their failure to influence, inspire or guide sections of the electorate. Many have found it difficult to resist the temptation of blaming the media for their own political ineptitude and failures.

The attack on mass culture indirectly targets the very idea of democracy itself. In an age where democracy is at least rhetorically accepted as the foundation for political life, it cannot be openly attacked without provoking a negative reaction. Calling into question mass culture and mass society achieves the objective of querying the moral authority of democracy in an indirect form.

In today's world, where an explicit language that touches on the superiority or inferiority of people is forbidden, arguments against democracy cannot be conducted in their classical aristocratic form. That is why discussions of mass man focus on people's role as victims of manipulation and of forces beyond their control.

Chapter 7

The psychological devaluation of the people

Political psychology has often served as a medium for diseasing the *demos*, and by implication, democracy itself. In the nineteenth century, psychologists developed theories of the crowd, which stressed the irrational and destructive behaviour of the urban mobs. A more sophisticated version of such theories emerged in the 1920s and 1930s, where people's psychological dispositions were blamed for the rise of authoritarianism and fascism. In the current era, citizens supporting so-called populist parties are diagnosed as possessing toxic authoritarian personalities.

As we have seen, arguments against democracy were historically based on an explicit moral critique, which condemned the masses as an essentially primitive and unintelligent force incapable of exercising reason. In the nineteenth century, moral condemnation was reframed through the language of the new science of psychology. The historian Reba Soffer argues that psychology should be seen as a constituent element of a new liberal elitist theory that developed as a response to the 'unreasonable and unpredictable behaviour of the new democracy'[1]. Soffer suggests that psychology provided liberal elitist theory with 'scientific' arguments about the incompatibility of democracy with the reality of people's behaviour.

Psychology's contribution to the silent war against democracy has been in serving to de-politicise and medicalise the behaviour of its target. Views that inspire and motivate popular movements are dismissed as the outcome of psychological pathologies – narcissism, irrationalism, deluded fantasy – rather than as legitimate political responses to public problems. Psychology has helped to reframe old arguments about the moral turpitude of the demos in a language that both normalises and naturalises its unfitness for a political role. In the twenty-first century, psychology continues to provide quasi-scientific resources to devalue the moral status of citizenship and democratic decision-making.

Psychology's political diagnosis of the popular mind

According to Graham Richards, social psychology begins with Gustave Le Bon's *The Crowd: A Study Of The Popular Mind* (1896)[2]. Industrial and political upheavals, such as the revolutions of 1848 and the Paris Commune, provided the context in which Le Bon elaborated his ideas, and policy-makers, scientists and intellectuals began to investigate the 'popular mind' and what they characterised as the 'personality of the people'. Crowd psychologists were in no doubt that the easily disturbed and volatile emotional state of the people undermined their ability to participate in public life in a responsible manner.

Le Bon, who was haunted by the experience of the French Revolution, regarded controlling the masses and taming public opinion as the main challenges facing modern society. His study of the crowd was not so much a work of detached analysis but a moral condemnation of the popular mind. According to his account, the condition of mass society wore away the historically acquired forms of civilised behaviour to expose the 'savage and primitive' survivals beneath. Le Bon believed that the traits that characterise the crowd are its 'impulsiveness, irritability, incapacity to reason, the absence of judgment of the critical spirit'[3]. Le Bon portrayed the supposedly irrational emotion of the crowd as a threat to a rationally-based social order.

Le Bon's reaction to the emergence of mass society ran in parallel with the explosion of studies of the crowd mind during the decades following the publication of *The Crowd*[4]. His views anticipated the sentiments of early twentieth-century psychoanalysts such as William McDougal and Sigmund Freud, who claimed that 'the people' still retained some of the destructive instincts of the primitive world. Numerous psychologists regarded the masses as irrational, unable to understand their own interests, and potentially volatile and dangerous.

The emerging discipline of psychology, through its theories of the 'crowd', played an important role in providing a narrative through which the alleged mismatch between rational institutions and an irrational public were most systematically expressed. The psychology of collective irrationality became an expression of both the conservative and the liberal reaction to the democratisation of public life. As the historian Robert Nye states:

> Collective psychology thus articulated a liberal critique of democratic tendencies in industrial societies with a facade of 'scientific' and clinical terminology that lent a certain respectability to its pronouncements[5].

Crowd psychology not only offered arguments for discrediting democracy. It also supplied 'scientific' arguments for the indispensability of strong elite leadership for dealing with the threat posed by the crowd, and techniques of manipulation and propaganda with which to influence and manage the emotions and behaviour of the people.

Psychological solutions for motivating the masses

The first 3 decades of the twentieth century saw an unprecedented interest in the development of techniques that could be used to influence the public's mind through new instruments of persuasion. The use of propaganda and manipulation is frequently associated with the behaviour of fascist, communist and totalitarian governments. In fact, all forms of government – even those that attempted to defend representative democracy

– developed an interest in harnessing psychology's potential for controlling mass behaviour. The turn towards psychological politics was driven by the hope that techniques of persuasion could relieve authorities of the burden of having to influence public opinion through political debate and discussion.

A special issue of the *Annals of the American Academy of Political and Social Science* in 1935 indicated that dictatorial regimes did not possess a monopoly on the use of thought control and techniques of psychological manipulation. In his introduction to this collection of essays on propaganda, Harwood Childs, a leading authority on public opinion, was blunt in his warning that the 'struggle for power, domestically and internationally, is in large part a struggle for control over the minds of men'. Success in this struggle did not depend on the force of ideas, but on the technical sophistication of propagandists. Childs argued that the 'groups which excel, whether official or unofficial, will be those most effectively implemented with the techniques and tools of opinion leadership'[6].

Child's statement on the struggle for 'control over the minds of men' was in part a reaction to the apparent effectiveness of dictatorial regimes in developing techniques of mass manipulation. His aim was to win the argument for accepting propaganda as a rational technique of governance. This point was forcefully promoted by the social psychologist Leonard Doob, who wrote a series of monographs advocating the virtues of propaganda, insisting that it 'is neither better nor worse than "rational" discourse'. As far as he was concerned, 'the simple emotional appeal, like statistical and dialectical arguments, may be put to good purposes as well as to bad'[7].

Doob's justification for using techniques of persuasion was that moral and ethical truths could not be relied on to prevail against falsehoods. With his collaborator, Edward Robinson, he wrote:

Whether one looks upon the psychological problem of modern social life as that of securing complete control over the sources of psychological influence, or whether one accepts the conception that only limiting controls should be exercised to define areas of free expression, there is no longer any possibility of escaping the problem on the ground that when truth and falsehood are turned loose against each other, truth will necessarily triumph. Too much of such "truth" is the dogma of those who have the power to issue decrees[8].

Scepticism about the authority of the truth was matched by the conviction that control of the public's mind through propaganda constituted a legitimate instrument for controlling public opinion.

The embrace of psychological manipulation techniques was, in turn, justified by the claim that a public moved mainly by irrational drives needed the guidance of rational expertise. Disillusionment with how representative democracy worked encouraged a quest for technical and psychological solutions to the problem of governance in the 1930s. However, the challenge posed by the Soviet Union, Nazi Germany and Fascist Italy intensified the demand for techniques of mass persuasion. The apparent success of totalitarian regimes in gaining the obedience of their citizens was frequently attributed to the success of psychological propaganda.

In the United States, Lasswell was in the forefront of calling for adoption of psychological techniques of propaganda. He praised the 'contribution of psychoanalysis' for throwing light on unconscious mass processes and concluded that as a result, 'the possibility of controlling mass insecurity by manipulating significant symbols has been put in new perspective[9]'. Lasswell appeared to be fascinated by the power of political manipulation, writing that the 'management of masses by propaganda has become one of the principal characteristics of our epoch'.

In this era, rulers who depended on bread and circuses were 'superseded by rulers who are adept at diverting, distracting, confusing, and dissipating the insecurities of the mass by the circulation of efficacious symbols'[10].

Lasswell believed that the emotions of the masses had become the focus for political intervention, and that psychiatry was an instrument of enlightened governance and the prevention of war. He portrayed psychologists as doctors who could cure, or at least neutralise, the emotional passions of the people, writing of the 'special province of political psychiatrists who seek to develop and to practice the politics of prevention' through 'devising ingenious expedients capable of discharging accumulated anxieties as harmlessly as possible'. Lasswell claimed that 'the political psychiatrist' now assumed responsibility for the 'task of mastering the source and mitigating the consequences of human insecurity in our unstable world'[11].

The advocacy of techniques of persuasion often expressed an anti-democratic creed that regarded propaganda, advertising techniques and the use of psychology as legitimate ways of gaining consensus. In the United States a fine line separated public education from propaganda. So in 1932, the US psychologist Horace B. English observed that social consensus could be easily forged 'by using the current psychological techniques of mass persuasion'. He stated that 'if the right catch-words are used, a group of emotions with a corresponding complex of ideas is so effectively aroused that reflection becomes impossible'[12].

Throughout the twentieth century, the authority of the science of psychology was used to call into question the capacity of the people to assume the role of responsible citizens. Political psychology, in particular, contained a powerful strain of anti-populist sentiment. To this day, it often conveys the argument that since the people are more likely to respond to appeals to emotion than rational arguments, the maintenance of stability and order requires the use of the psychological management of public life.

Post-World War II: Consolidation of liberalism's fear of populism

In the post-Second World War era, the tendency to psychologise the problems faced by liberal democracy gained a powerful momentum. Sections of the Left regarded the psychology of the working class as inconsistent with the goal of achieving a tolerant democratic society. Some of the leading intellectuals associated with the British Labour Party adopted a negative view of the psychological sensibility of the working class. In 1945, at a Fabian conference on 'The Psychological and Sociological Problems of Modern Socialism' in Oxford, a leading party intellectual, Evan Durbin, explained that, 'people were far more wicked, ie mentally ill, than was commonly supposed...they put their wickedness into their social life: and as a whole were all very sick and very stupid'[13].

Durbin's pessimistic view of the people led him for a time to advocate selective breeding and eugenics. His colleague, Anthony Crosland, soon to be a leading minister in the Labour government of the 1960s, noted that the working-class people he encountered in the army were in the mass 'rather like a lot of wild animals' but when alone they were 'almost as human' as 'most middle class people'[14].

During the 1940s and 1950s, popular opinion became increasingly psychologised. Psychologists began to hint that public opinion, particularly in its populist form, tended to be under the influence of prejudiced, authoritarian and illiberal sentiments. The current tendency to medicalise populism as irrational and sick is closely based on the theory and analysis advanced by associates of the Frankfurt School. Almost everything that has been said about the mindset of the twenty-first century populist can be found in a series of publications in the 1950s around their theme of 'the Authoritarian Personality'.

The main author of the concept of an Authoritarian Personality was Adorno. Despite his supposed association with cultural Marxism, Adorno possessed a classical elitist contempt towards the masses and mass culture. In a nutshell, his argument was that the masses suffer from psychological deficits, which make them unable to understand their own interest. These insecure individuals possess a personality type that is drawn towards authoritarian leaders and movements. According to Adorno and his colleagues, such personality deficits were associated with individuals drawn towards right-wing political ideals, in contrast to those with anti-authoritarian personality dispositions, who were characteristically on the Left.

Adorno adopted a medicalised narrative to assess right-wing and authoritarian trends. In his discussion of 'Vaccines Against Authoritarianism', he advocated 'making the best possible use of the insights of depth psychology'. He also suggested that it was necessary to grasp the 'techniques of the enemy' since it 'might derive from them, as it were, vaccines against antidemocratic indoctrination'[15]. Ostensibly, Adorno stood for protecting democracy from its opponents. But his call to adopt the techniques of the enemy and rely on psychological vaccines to immunise people from being drawn towards authoritarian ideas reflected the anti-democratic impulse of a social engineer. It indicated an attitude of a deep-seated sense of mistrust towards the behaviour of the people – an attitude that characterises all the historical forms of anti-democratic thought.

Some observers have drawn attention to what they saw as a strongly politicised agenda that underpinned the concept of an Authoritarian Personality. The social critic Christopher Lasch argued that by equating mental health with left-wing politics and associating right-wing politics with an invented 'authoritarian' pathology, the 'goal was to eliminate authoritarianism' by 'subjecting the American people to what amounted to collective psychotherapy – by treating them as inmates of an insane asylum'[16].

A review of the age-long ideological war against democracy suggests that, its scientific pretensions notwithstanding, contentions about the authoritarian disposition of sections of the public were a new version of ancient arguments about the tyranny of the majority. In different guises, this argument continues to recur in political psychology's engagement with populist movements. The most influential advocate of the medicalisation of the populism was the American historian Richard Hofstadter. His 1964 study, *The Paranoid Style of American Politics*, offered an analysis of the diseases of populism that is still evoked to this day. He self-consciously acknowledged that he borrowed the 'clinical term' paranoia as a 'pejorative' diagnosis of a political style that he despised[17].

In an interesting study of Cold War political culture, Ron Robin suggests that psychology became an alternative to ideology as both an explanation and as a tool for dealing with competing arguments[18]. During this period, the imperative of psychologising populist individuals and movements transcended the conventional political divide. In the liberal literature of the Cold War, the tendency to attribute psychological deficits to both left and right-wing populism was closely linked to a sense of distrust of the working classes. Elite apprehensions towards populism were linked to the belief that the mental outlook of the 'lower classes' was distorted by its brutal upbringing. It was claimed that the emotional outlook of the working class created a propensity to adopt anti-democratic and illiberal causes. The comments of the American political scientist Seymour Martin Lipset, a leading voice on this subject during the Cold War, are paradigmatic in this respect:

> To sum up, the lower-class individual is likely to have been exposed to punishment, lack of love, and a general atmosphere of tension and aggression since early childhood –

all experiences which tend to produce deep-rooted hostilities expressed by ethnic prejudice, political authoritarianism, and chiliastic transvaluational religion[19].

The contrast drawn between the emotionally refined middle classes and the emotionally illiterate working classes was also forcefully drawn by Hans Eysenck, a well-known British psychologist. Eysenck claimed that 'middle-class Conservatives are more tender-minded than working-class Conservatives; middle-class Liberals more tender-minded than working-class Liberals; middle-class Socialists more tender-minded than working-class Socialists and even middle-class communists more tender-minded than working-class communists'[20]. Almost 60 years on, the same methodology is still used to medicalise the populist personality. A 2019 study of the populist personality by Nai and Martinex concluded:

> Largely confirming our expectations, our analyses show that populists score significantly lower on agreeableness, emotional stability and conscientiousness; right-wing populists score particularly low on this last trait. At the same time, populists score significantly and substantially higher on the 'dark' traits of narcissism, psychopathy and Machiavellianism, but also on extraversion[21].

In all but name this 2019 study predictably restates the anti-populist conclusions drawn by the authors of the *Authoritarian Personality* in the 1950s.

A long time before the emergence of the twenty-first century populist movements, political psychology developed a language and mindset through which its behaviour and outlook could be comprehended. The tendency to stigmatise populist politics as a symptom of psychological disorder and irrationalism gained momentum during the 1950s and 1960s. According to one account, for liberal intellectuals of the 1950s, 'populism became the paradigmatic case of American-style xenophobia'[22]. In *The Populist Persuasion*, Michael Kazin noted that in the United States during the Cold War, populism became the 'great fear of liberal intellectuals', who blamed mass democracy and an 'authoritarian' and 'irrational' working class for being easily swayed by the demagogy of McCarthyism. Whereas 'formerly liberals had worried about the decline of popular participation in politics' now 'they began to wonder whether "apathy" might not be a blessing in disguise', noted Lasch[23].

The celebration of apathy by Cold War liberal theorists represented a remarkable departure from the significance that the rhetoric of democracy attached to the value of public participation. This reversal in attitude towards the involvement of citizens in public life was now justified on the ground that stable democratic governance required widespread apathy and indifference to politics. Advocates of the virtue of political apathy argued that 'if the uninformed masses participate in large numbers, democratic self-restraint will break down and peaceful competition among the elites, the central element in the elitist theory, will become impossible'[24]. In a monograph titled 'In Defense of Apathy', British academic Wyndraeth Morris-Jones asserted that 'the general theme of the Duty to Vote belong properly to the totalitarian camp and are out of place in the vocabulary of liberal democracy'[25].

In effect, at times, psychology acquired the form of anti-democratic ideology. It encouraged anti-populist activists to claim that there was no point in debating individuals whose ideas were not only wrong but also sick. Herbert Marcuse argued that freedom of speech was pointless in a society where so many people were infected with mental corruption. In 1965, he demanded 'the withdrawal of toleration of speech and assembly from groups and movements which promote aggressive policies, armaments, chauvinism, discrimination on the grounds of race and religion, or which oppose the extension of public services, social security, medical care, etc'[26]. Marcuse unashamedly advocated the adoption of the policy of 'repressive tolerance', which meant intolerance towards those with whose views he disagreed. Repressive tolerance advocated the use of psychological indoctrination to cure people of their sick ideas.

Return of the pathologisation of the crowd

In the current era, the crude language of nineteenth century crowd psychology has given way to a more restrained diagnosis of the mental health deficits allegedly associated with populist and extremist behaviour. Nevertheless, displays of public emotions and populist aspirations are often portrayed as the consequence of dysfunctional personality traits. In this way, the representation of popular movements continues to be both psychologised and depoliticised.

As one commentator argues, extremism is not so much a political as a psychological problem. Hence, supporters of Brexit are characteristically prone to anger, resentment, self-pity and possess a powerful sense of victimhood[27]. People who supposedly vote the wrong way are not merely criticised but also psychologically diagnosed; a psychological diagnosis is seamlessly interwoven with moral condemnation. As the political commentator Ivan Krastev noted:

> The rise of populist parties as a rule invites psychological or even psychoanalytical interpretations. Commentators consciously or unconsciously are tempted to analyze populism in terms of "the return of the repressed," "traumas," "frustrations," and "status anxieties"[28].

Psychological explanations of the motives and behaviour of people supporting Brexit and other populist causes invariably insist that they are not driven by rational calculation. According to *Time Magazine*, 'psychology made the Brexit vote inevitable' – psychologists 'haven't been the slightest bit surprised' by the outcome of the referendum, which was 'primarily a function of the irrational ways of the human mind'[29]. The statement that psychology made Brexit 'inevitable' allows supporters of this outlook to ignore the very real aspiration for democratic control that inspired a significant section of the electorate.

The simplistic use of psychology as a pseudo-scientific form of polemic disturbs some psychologists who take their profession seriously. Though he is unsympathetic to the Brexit vote, Michael Smith, author of *The Psychology of Brexit*, is concerned that 'remain-leaning pundits attribute Brexit to psychopathology – a kind of madness – because they simply cannot imagine how a rational Leave-voting person might feel'[30].

It is not simply an absence of imagination, but an intense sensibility of insecurity about those who embrace a different set of cultural values, that explains the return of the ugly language of nineteenth-century crowd psychology.

The aftermath of the Brexit Referendum saw statements such as, 'Brexit was fuelled by irrational xenophobia, not economic grievances,' draw attention to the primitive impulses that allegedly dominate the populist mindset[31]. Numerous commentators claimed that rage, not reason, motivates citizens whose voting behaviour they despise. Simplistic versions of neuroscience have been recruited to reinforce this anti-democratic narrative. According to neuroscientist Douglas Fields, the election of Donald Trump is best understood as the neuroscience of rage: 'To understand this election you must understand the brain's threat detection mechanism'[32].

The re-emergence of the language of crowd psychology is inevitably accompanied by the ancient tendency to regard the people as a mob. Following Trump's election, the commentator Matthew Parris wrote in *The Spectator* of his fear that we are no longer 'keeping the mob from the gates'[33]. Others use more subtle language to describe voters who are 'literally' ignorant. Professor Jason Brennan invented the term 'low-information white people' as a synonym for what used to be referred to as 'white thrash' in the dictionary of the snobbish elites[34].

In the nineteenth century, crowd psychology not only invalidated the political capacities of the lower class – it also sought to de-humanise their instincts and behaviour. They were portrayed as a primitive race, different to the refined civilised behaviour of their cultural superiors. Back in 1872, the leading commentator Walter Bagehot compared the English poor to faraway savages, stating that, 'the lower classes in civilised countries, like all classes in uncivilised countries are clearly wanting in the nicer part of those feelings which, taken together, we call the *sense* of morality'[35].

Bagehot would have understood and sympathised with the predicaments of groups of Italian aristocrats, businessmen and cultural figures having dinner on a Roman roof terrace after the success of populist parties in Italy's general election of 2017. A reporter for *The Times* observed as they sat around 'glumly digesting events', a lawyer in attendance declared that the voters were 'beasts' and 'anthropologically different'[36].

The psychologisation of citizens' political behaviour forecloses the possibility that a clash of conflicting views, a genuine open debate between adherents of different ideas and policies, can have beneficial results for society. As we will see in the next chapter, this pessimistic diagnosis constitutes an indirect call for the displacement of democratic decision-making by experts, technocrats and social engineers.

Chapter 8

The political sacralisation of expertise

The flipside of psychology's representation of the people as immature and irrational was its demand that decision-making should be managed by experts and educated elites. As we have seen, historically the wisdom of the few has often been starkly counterposed to the ignorance of the masses. However, with the rise of representative democracy, and the recognition that a stable political order required legitimation by popular consent, there was a shift in the way that the necessity for expert authority was posed. The key challenge faced by advocates of expert authority was how to reconcile democratic participation with deference to the political wisdom of experts.

At a symposium of the Aristotelian Society in 1908, philosophers expressed the hope that a system of representative democracy would retain a place for what Bernard Bosanquet called the 'Platonic statesman-expert at his best'[1]. However, by this point in time the case for expert authority could not be convincingly promoted in its classical form. Science, and in particular psychology, came to the rescue, with its claim that the complex problems facing modern society required the specialist knowledge of experts[2].

From the standpoint of upholding the values of democracy, the problem is not expertise and science as such. Society depends on the development of science and it relies on the professional knowledge of its experts to deal with the many challenges it faces. Experts have a vital role to play in a democratic political system – but their role is a technical or administrative one. The problem discussed in this chapter is the trend towards the politicisation of expertise and the tendency to endow experts with a monopoly over decision-making in a variety of areas that crucially affect everyone. This authorisation of expertise becomes a problem when their monopoly over decision-making violates the fundamental norms of democratic accountability.

The trend towards politicisation of expertise can be understood through understanding the distinction between **epistemic** and **epistemocratic** authority. Epistemic authority is 'that which is ascribed to the possessor of specialized knowledge, skills, or expertise'[3]. This form of authority works through deference to doctors on medical matters, and to lawyers on legal affairs. Epistemocratic authority 'by contrast, refers to the claim of one class, group, or person to rule another by virtue of the former's possessing specialized authority not available to the latter'. As Terrence Ball explains:

> Epistemocratic authority is therefore conceptually parasitic upon epistemic authority. Or, to put it slightly differently, epistemocratic authority attempts to assimilate political authority to the non-political epistemic authority of the technician or expert[4].

Ball claims that the conceptual distinction between political rule and expert authority in modern society has become 'blurred if not meaningless'.

In effect, the epistemocratic imperative extends the claim of expertise to the domain of political and public life. It assimilates moral and political issues to 'the paradigm of epistemic authority' and asserts that 'politics and ethics are activities in which there are experts'[5]. The influence exercised by epistemocratic authority today is shown by the constant slippage between scientific advice and moral and political exhortation on issues as different as global warming and child rearing. The zenith of epistemocratic authority was achieved during the coronavirus epidemic. 'No message, statement or utterance can be made by a representative of the government without being foreshadowed and subsequently enmeshed within the golden phrase that is "following the expert advice we are receiving"', noted an academic commentary on the use of expertise during the Covid-19 crisis[6].

The rise of the expert

Since the eighteenth century, most Western societies have attempted to reconcile popular sovereignty with parliamentary sovereignty, through a form of representative democracy. However, for many anti-majoritarian commentators, even parliamentary sovereignty is too directly influenced by the will of the people. Consequently, they often prefer to look to expert-led institutions, such as the judiciary, or transnational bodies such as the International Monetary Fund or the European Union, to minimise the influence of popular opinion on the deliberation of decision-makers.

The politicisation of expertise emerged in response to the political instability confronting nineteenth-century societies in newly-industrialising European societies, when the traditional forms of oligarchical rule were on the defensive and forced to make concessions to demands for political reform. At a time when traditional sources of legitimation appeared exhausted, science seemed to possess a singular capacity to provide society with an authoritative guide to the future. Sections of political elites hoped that science and expertise possessed a unique capacity to gain the people's deference, which was otherwise absent in public life. It was in this vein that in 1833, Edward Bulwer Lytton, a Whig member of parliament, called for a 'government of knowledge'.

Politicians and educated elites drew on the authority of science to legitimate their decisions and claims. They devoted considerable energy towards constructing their authority as the possessors of knowledge, wisdom and superior insight. The question at issue was whether their knowledge would be recognised as authoritative by the rest of society. Those of a conservative disposition tended to be pessimistic about the capacity of the elites to maintain cultural and intellectual authority. Writing in this vein, Tocqueville expressed concern that the influence of an egalitarian ethos led to rejection of the 'authority of learned elites'[7].

Distrust towards the opinion of the people led some devotees of expertise to adopt a coercive approach to public debate and discussion. The French philosopher Auguste Comte insisted that since the necessity for citizens to defer to experts was self-evident, the people needed to be made to listen to their wisdom. He asserted that 'the critical spirit' is 'directly contrary to that which ought to reign in scientific politics'[8]. According to Comte, the views of science and expertise were beyond legitimate questioning and challenge by members of the public. Although such an absolutist version of technocratic authority was rarely expressed in such open form, many advocates of expertise shared Comte's assumptions.

J.S. Mill opted for a version of expert authority, a *clerisy*, that distanced itself from what he characterised as Comte's 'spiritual despotism'[9]. Mill's writings on the capacity of expert rulers to influence public opinion tended to fluctuate between a mood of restrained optimism and one of sober concern. Writing in the *Westminster Review* in April 1849, he defended the 1848 French Revolution but argued that the legislative activity should be reserved for 'the intellectual elite of France'. In line with his previous views, Mill suggested that it is not for the people to govern, but only to choose a well-qualified assembly to govern for them; it is not for the assembly to make laws, but only to see that they are made by a panel of experts[10].

Arguments for the institutionalisation of epistemocratic authority coexisted with the recognition that there were clear limits to the purview of expertise. There was no possibility of avoiding the gradual expansion of the franchise, and a balance had to be found between the authority of expertise and that of popular representation. In the late-nineteenth and early-twentieth centuries, the most enthusiastic supporters of the sacralisation of expertise were the New Liberals in the United Kingdom and the progressive movement in the United States[11]. The attraction of new liberals and socialists to the authorisation of experts was noted by the British jurist Albert Dicey, who observed that the 'socialist's ideal is a state ruled by officials or experts who are socialists'[12], and praised 'the socialist' for escaping 'the folly of idealising the people'. Many social democrats in Western and northern Europe believed that the expert or the social engineer offered the best guarantee of sound administration and management of public life. During the 1930s and 1940s, social-democratic parties became enthusiastic supporters of social engineering.

In the United States, progressivism was drawn towards the advocacy of social engineering on the grounds that damaging political conflict and party politics could be overcome if the partisan politicians were replaced by experts[13]. During the early part of the twentieth century, the idealisation of social engineering acquired great influence over American political life. This period is often referred to as the 'age of the expert', when political reformers invested their hopes in displacing party-political conflict with the wisdom of social engineers. As Michael Tanner, a critic of this development, outlined, progressivism 'caused many Americans to believe that "experts" were required to solve most problems, and that only government could provide the needed expertise'. He added that before the progressive era, 'the purpose of government had been seen as protecting individual rights. Now, government was seen as a problem solver'[14].

During the 1930s, the achievement of reform through social engineering became the objective of the intellectual wing of the American Democratic Party. The cult of expertise gained prominence during President Franklin Roosevelt's New Deal. With the rise of fascism and the consolidation of Stalin's regime in Russia, the idealisation of a government of administrators and experts gained influence. It was paralleled with a loss of faith in democracy and the ability of the public to face the challenge posed by totalitarian regimes.

This sentiment was forcefully expounded by Walter Shepard, President of the American Political Science Association, when he baldly stated that the idea that 'government springs from, and is dependent upon, the will of the people cannot withstand the analysis of modern criticism'[15]. Although he recognised that the 'electorate has its role to play in modern government', that role is a matter of 'practical expediency' to be decided on pragmatic grounds. Shepard called for the abandonment of the theory of popular sovereignty, proposing instead a model of a technocratic political system, based on planning and education and run by men with 'brains'. In such a political regime the people would have a limited minor role to play. Shepard wanted to 'lose the halo' surrounding the electorate to give 'way to a system of educational and other tests which will exclude the ignorant, the uninformed, and the anti-social elements which hitherto have so frequently controlled elections'. His vision was of a modern technocracy run by experts[16].

Experts as saviours of democracy

From the 1930s onwards, and especially after the end of the Second World War, advocates of social engineering and of expert administrators were forced to make concessions to the growing influence of democracy. In Western societies, especially in the Anglo-American world, governments drew on the inspirational properties of freedom and democracy to counter the ideological appeals of the Axis powers. Sections of the political establishment of the Allied nations may have been sceptical about the working of mass democracy, but they relied on the mobilising power of the ethos of freedom and equality, and portrayed the defeat of fascism as the downfall of the movement most associated with an explicit rejection of parliamentary democracy. For this reason, after the Second World War it was unthinkable for any political movement – including the communist parties – to openly express any explicitly anti-democratic sentiments. Apologists for Stalin's regime frequently asserted that the constitution of the Soviet Union was the most democratic in the world. As for the West, its self-chosen description of itself as the Free World was incessantly coupled to its claim to uphold a democratic way of life. During the Cold War, both sides of the conflict flaunted their democratic credentials.

Yet the official endorsement of democracy as the defining political philosophy of Western societies was rarely backed up by strong conviction and intellectual force. In the post-Second World War era, policy-makers and their experts continued to equate the exercise of democracy with a problem: the capacity of the public to handle its freedoms and democratic rights in a responsible manner. In particular, popular sovereignty was castigated as an unreliable institution, and frequently dismissed as an outdated concept that simply had no relevance in a modern mass society.

The experience of the Second World War may have boosted the authority of democracy, but in a form that was unapologetically elitist. In this historical context, the political role of expertise altered in order to ensure that its exercise did not directly come into conflict with the commanding influence of the ethos of democracy. Expertise was promoted, not only as an instrument for keeping democratic excesses at bay, but also as a means of guiding and, if necessary, revitalising it. Social scientists and propagandists were charged with the task of guiding public opinion away from the influence of radical totalitarian ideologies. This project of using political expertise for educating members of the public to understand and appreciate democratic citizenship was promoted on the grounds that it was necessary to prevent people from succumbing to totalitarian temptations.

Unlike earlier forms of explicitly anti-democratic ideologies of expert authority, a new version sought to project the expert as a source of democratic enlightenment. Like the previous version of expert-led social engineering theories, this new one concurred with the premise that the average person was incapable of making rational choices and was entirely at the mercy of the manipulators of the mass media. However, there was now the possibility that the average person could be redeemed through the intervention of an enlightened expert. As the historian Daria Frezza explained, from the perspective of this theory, 'the experts' crucial role' was 'to guide the average citizen through an ever more complex social network that deprived individuals of their autonomy'[17].

The advocacy of democratic education was promoted on the grounds that science, and psychological techniques in particular, could be used to curb the irrational and dangerous manifestations of mass democracy. In this way democracy could be recast as 'government for the people by enlightened and responsible elites'[18]. Edward Bernays, often referred to as the 'father of public relations', played an important role in attempting to reconcile the democratic aspirations of people in the post-Second World War setting with a model of government by an enlightened democratically-minded elite. His objective was to achieve what he characterised as the 'engineering of consent'.

Bernays, like other supporters of social engineering, recognised that no government could aspire to legitimacy unless it could claim to rule by popular consent. His aim was not to leave the emergence of consent to chance, but to influence it so that its ideals and objectives became harmonious with those of an enlightened elite. Bernays justified the need to 'engineer' consent on the grounds that 'it is sometimes impossible to reach joint decisions based on an understanding of facts by all the people'[19]. According to Bernays, the reason for the failure to reach decisions based on facts was because many people could not understand them:

> The average American adult has only six years of schooling behind him. With pressing crises and decisions to be faced, a leader frequently cannot wait for the people to arrive at even general understanding. In certain cases, democratic leaders must play their part in leading the public through the engineering of consent to socially constructive goals and values[20].

In other words, since often leaders cannot wait until the people come to an understanding of the issues at stake, consent needed to be engineered.

The engineering of consent relied on education and on what Bernays referred to euphemistically as 'other available techniques'. Bernays underlined the importance of his approach by indicating that 'even in a society of a perfectionist educational standard' the 'engineering of consent would still be essential'[21]. Unlike some of his colleagues, Bernays was relatively optimistic about the possibility of overcoming the people's intellectual deficits through education and guidance. Yet, as someone who was wholeheartedly devoted to the project of manipulating public opinion, he failed to consider the implication of the idea of artificially engineering consent. Such a notion of consent is entirely alien to one that comes about through public debate and democratic discussion. It not only short-circuits the crystallisation of a genuine, democratically created public consent on the issues of the day, but also calls into question the very value of public deliberation.

Projects that are devoted to the engineering of consent deprive democracy of its inner creative content by devaluing the significance of deliberation and, in some cases, seeking to colonise it. Since the 1980s, expert saviours of democracy have developed new techniques for forging opinion in order to claim that they represent the consent of the people. They advocate a technique, which they disingenuously characterise as *deliberative democracy*, as a medium for ensuring that people arrive at the decision desired by their social engineers. Deliberative democracy is often supported on the grounds that it provides a small group environment conducive for people to change their mind and adopt the ethos favoured by the forum's organisers. Deliberation is favoured because it can act as a vehicle for transmitting the outlook of the organisers.

The process of socially engineered deliberation depends on 'procedures, techniques and methods' worked out by experts[22]. The procedure itself is administered by professional facilitators whose rules are designed to assist the management of individuals participating in the deliberative democracy workshops. This is not a forum where the participants interact as equals. Skilled facilitators are employed to create the right kind of environment and the desirable outcomes. A discussant of the virtues of 'citizens' juries' notes that it relies on 'trained moderators' who ensure 'fair proceedings'[23]. Yet without a hint of self-consciousness, this highly manipulative environment is endorsed as a superior alternative to 'liberal institutions' which supposedly encourage the passivity of citizens[24]. What we have is the pretence of deliberation and the reality of manipulation.

Some advocates of deliberative democracy explicitly regard it as a form of social engineering through which the participants can be manipulated to arrive at the 'correct' outcome. They see it as a vehicle for the emotional management of the participants, fearing that if a group is allowed the freedom to develop its own emotional dynamic, the wrong decisions may be made. 'In extreme circumstances, we may judge that a group came to the wrong conclusion since its collective emotions had too strong an influence on its deliberations,' they note. There is little scope here for genuine political debate and dialogue. People can deliberate as long as they arrive at the 'right conclusion'[25].

It is a sign of the times that a procedure that could come straight from Orwell's *Nineteen Eighty-Four* can be represented as an enlightened alternative to representative democracy. The assumption that the professional facilitator has the moral authority to determine how people should emote is symptomatic of a patronising orientation towards the 'deliberators'.

The dogma of complexity

Unlike a century ago, the authority of expertise can no longer be justified through explicit statements about mental and intellectual deficits of the public. Most experts use a more euphemistic language to draw attention to what they regard as the irrational emotions of the people. But increasingly, expertise is justified as something that is good in its own right. The main argument for supporting the authority of political expertise is the claim that we live in an increasingly complex and rapidly changing world. Through highlighting the difficulty of grasping the complexity facing decision-makers, citizens' ability to deal with important issues is called into question.

The fetishisation of complexity implicitly devalues the role of democratic deliberation. For example, opponents of recent referenda within EU countries argue that issues facing the public are too complex to be grasped by members of the public. This argument was widely expressed during the debates that followed the referenda on the EU constitution in France and the Netherlands. Margot Wallstrom, the then vice-president of the European Commission, commented in her blog that the constitution is a 'complex issue to vote on', which can confuse many citizens, leading them to 'use a referendum to answer a question that was not put to them'. Similar views were communicated after the referendum in which British people supported Brexit.

The claim that the issues were too complex for the people to grasp constitutes the principal justification for endowing expertise with political authority. Some leading environmentalists argue that complex ecological problems are far too difficult to be left to the unpredictable outcome of democratic decision-making. They assert that unlike scientists and experts, who take a long view of environmental threats, a short-sighted public will resist taking the steps necessary to save the planet[26].

There has even been a return of the old class supremacist arguments, which regard citizens who display mistrust towards political expertise, or who vote 'the wrong way', as intellectually and mentally deficient. According to a blog published by the prestigious London School of Economics, the distrust displayed by voters towards expertise in the UK and the US is evidence of their anti-intellectualism. The author of this essay stated that his research of survey data indicates that 'anti-intellectualism is linked to voters' support for candidates and political movements that are sceptical of expertise'[27]. It has also been widely argued that sceptics of expertise have lower levels of verbal intelligence than citizens who place their trust in experts. Here, we see the latest version of crowd psychology's narrative regarding the mental inferiority of the masses.

Plato's disdain for the *demos* and his advocacy of the authority of the expert has reappeared in a modern form in anti-populist cultural script. So it is not surprising that during the Brexit Referendum campaign, anti-populist commentators reacted with outrage to the statement made by the Conservative cabinet minister Michael Gove in which he stated: 'I think the people of this country have had enough of experts with organisations from acronyms saying that they know what is best and getting it consistently wrong.' The palpable sense of horror with which the anti-populist media responded to this statement indicated that from its standpoint, the authority of the expert stood between civilisation and the dreaded populist masses.

According to the narrative of anti-populism, the greatest sin of this movement is that it is prepared to question the judgement of the expert. In a tone of disbelief, two leading American political scientists, Pippa Norris and Ronald Inglehart, observed that populists embrace the voice of 'ordinary citizens' even 'when at odds with expert judgements – including those of elected representatives and judges, scientists, scholars, journalists and commentators'[28]! If that is the case, the anti-democratic hierarchical pyramid that situates the expert at the top and 'ordinary citizens' at the bottom, is turned upside down when epistemocractic authority is rejected.

If not the expert, who will exercise authority over the *demos*? This was a question that was formulated by Socrates a long time before the emergence of the current anti-populist cultural script. The conviction that the people are morally and intellectually inferior to their enlightened superiors constitutes the historical foundation of the anti-populist imagination. Since the emergence of popular populist movements during the past decade, arguments about upholding the sanctity of expertise have become increasingly shrill. Some opponents of populism were pleased that Covid-19 provided an opportunity for otherwise ignorant people to appreciate the importance of expertise. However, after a while, the constant refrain by politicians that they are doing what the scientists tell them began to wear thin. Even some of the experts became frustrated with politicians constantly hiding behind scientists in order to appear authoritative. 'As a scientist, I hope I never again hear the phrase "based on the best science and evidence" spoken by a politician,' stated Devi Sridhar, chair of global public health at the University of Edinburgh[29].

The willingness with which politicians outsourced their authority to the experts during the Covid-19 pandemic drew attention to their aversion to democratic accountability. In the next chapter we explore how this outsourcing of political authority has become a normal practice designed to insulate governments and institutions from the pressure of popular opinion.

Chapter 9

Democracy without the demos

Since the end of the Second World War, the formal idealisation of democracy has coexisted with mistrust about how people would use their political power. In response to this fear, the political classes adopted the twin-track strategy of insulating their institutions from direct popular pressure, and de-politicising decision-making through the use of expert, judicial and non-governmental organisations.

The post-1945 era has also seen the outsourcing of decision-making to a constantly growing number of international bodies. As I explain later in this chapter, these global organisations displace the national public sphere as a site of decision-making and are used to protect governments from the potentially destabilising impact of popular pressure. Through taking over decision-making from elected politicians, they undermine the role of representatives and the authority of representative democracy. Their aim is a democracy without the demos.

Defensive democracy

The concept of defensive or militant democracy was originally developed during the 1930s by the German political scientist Karl Loewenstein, in response to the threat posed by extremist authoritarian movements. Militant democracy is a form of governance that self-consciously uses undemocratic instruments to protect a liberal-democratic constitution from the supposed emotionalism of the popular mind. Loewenstein made a clear distinction between emotional and rational forms of governance, asserting that a rational form of governance relied on insulating the institutions of the state from the 'verdict of the people':

A pertinent illustration chosen from the experience of a democracy may clarify the vital difference between constitutional and emotional methods of government. The solution of the recent political crisis in England by the cabinet and the Commons was sought through rational means. To have left the issue to the verdict of the people would have been resorting to emotional methods, although general elections are manifestly a perfectly legitimate device of constitutional government[1].

Loewenstein believed that democratic institutions could be easily manipulated by fascist techniques of manipulation. He feared that since liberalism could not match the emotional appeal of fascism, what he characterised as 'democratic fundamentalism' posed a danger to the prevailing political order:

They [the fascists] exploit the tolerant confidence of democratic ideology that in the long run truth is stronger than falsehood, that the spirit asserts itself against force. Democracy was unable to forbid the enemies of its very existence the use of democratic instrumentalities. Until very recently, democratic fundamentalism and legalistic blindness were unwilling to realize that the mechanism of democracy is the Trojan horse by which the enemy enters the city[2].

The evocation of a Trojan horse to underline the perils of an unregulated democratic public sphere spoke to a profound sense of unease towards the masses. It also highlighted a lack of confidence in the ability of a democratically-minded constituency to uphold and defend the truth against falsehood.

Loewenstein explicitly endorsed an illiberal defence of liberal democracy. His was a social engineering approach, which regarded the psychology of the popular mind as the terrain on which fascism flourished. 'In order definitely to overcome the danger of Europe's going wholly fascist, it would be necessary to remove the causes, that is, to change the mental structure of this age of the masses and of rationalized emotion,' he wrote[3]. To achieve this objective, Loewenstein was prepared to opt for what he called 'authoritarian democracy':

> Perhaps the time has come when it is no longer wise to close one's eyes to the fact that liberal democracy, suitable, in the last analysis, only for the political aristocrats among the nations, is beginning to lose the day to the awakened masses. Salvation of the absolute values of democracy is not to be expected from abdication in favor of emotionalism, utilized for wanton or selfish purposes by self-appointed leaders, but by deliberate transformation of obsolete forms and rigid concepts into the new instrumentalities of "disciplined," or even – let us not shy from the word – "authoritarian," democracy[4].

Loewenstein's embrace of authoritarian democracy highlights the ease with which liberal elitism periodically adopts illiberal solutions in an attempt to neutralise its opponents. The statement, that liberal democracy is only suitable for the 'political aristocrats among the nations', implicitly calls into question its relevance for modern life. It suggests that for most nations, democracy is an inappropriate form of governance. Thus, for Loewenstein, there was no contradiction between seeking to preserve democracy with the use of undemocratic methods[5].

Loewenstein's distrust of popular sovereignty, and his preference for an aristocratic form of authoritarian democracy, was widely shared by policy-makers charged with the post-Second World War political reconstruction of Western Europe. The twenty-first century version of militant democracy has emerged in response to populism, not fascism – but it, too, wants to protect democracy by using essentially undemocratic means.

One recent example of this approach is a teaching kit directed at young people, and recently published by the Council of Europe. Pointing to the challenge presented by nationalist parties, the teaching kit warns that, 'it may be necessary to limit the right to freedom of expression of certain groups, despite the importance of this right to the democratic process'[6].

Protecting democracy from itself

Post-war European constitutional settlements sought to limit the role of parliament through assigning significant powers to the judiciary and newly constructed constitutional courts. Technocratic institutions also gained significant influence, especially through the medium of the new and evolving European Union.

The project of managing democracy to prevent a return to the bad old days of the interwar years was pursued most systematically in West Germany. There, the aim of the 1949 Basic Law was to prevent the recurrence of dictatorship. The reconstruction of Germany was guided by a commitment to limiting the influence of majoritarian democracy and popular sovereignty through providing the non-elected Constitutional Court with significant powers. It also gave the government far-reaching powers to ban and prosecute movements it deemed extremist. In Germany, the institutionalisation of 'defensive democracy' was self-consciously designed to 'protect the Germans from themselves'[7].

The ethos of protecting democracy from the people dictated the behaviour of political elites throughout Europe As one political scientist remarked, 'insulation from popular pressures and, more broadly, a deep distrust of popular sovereignty, underlay not just the beginnings of European integration, but the political reconstruction of Western Europe after 1945 in general'[8]. Motivated by the imperative of avoiding the upheavals of the interwar era and by an intense sense of suspicion of mass behaviour, the European elites 'fashioned a highly *constrained* form of democracy, deeply imprinted with a distrust of popular sovereignty – in fact, even a distrust of traditional parliamentary sovereignty'[9]. In many instances, law-making shifted from the public, parliamentary and a democratic political process to the courts.

In recent decades, judicial activism has accelerated further, and judgments handed down by the courts are often able to override the decisions taken by democratically elected parliaments and governments. The politicisation of the judiciary and its adoption of an interventionist high profile in public life is particularly widespread in the Anglo-American sphere. Judicial oversight of political decision-making not only limits the effectiveness of executive judgement, but also increasingly projects the courts as the possessors of an authority that trumps those of an elected executive. As one study notes: the US Supreme Court, 'has set itself up as an unelected superlegislature, decreeing that policies in one area after another, from regulation of abortion and marriage to campaign finance regulation, belong in the realm of inviolable constitutional rights and must be determined by life-tenured, unelected federal judges, rather than democratic legislatures or citizens initiatives'[10].

In Britain, the expansion of judicial activism, and particularly judicial review, since the 1970s is one of the most significant developments in this nation's public life. During the past 3 decades, the judiciary has come to play a key role in the promotion of constitutional reform. One critic of this development, the former Labour Home Secretary David Blunkett, wrote that judicial review has 'rapidly become an entirely new arm of our constitution, operated by judges, through judges, and without any redress or accountability to Parliament'[11].

The expanded involvement of the judiciary in political matters has not gone unnoticed. Supreme Court judge Lord Sumption, in his November 2013 lecture on 'The Limits of Law', warned of the growing 'tendency to convert political questions into legal ones', and drew attention to the prominent role played by single-issue and lobbying groups in the pursuit of judicial activism. 'Single-interest pressure groups, who stand behind a great deal of public law litigation', he argued, have 'no interest in policy areas other than their own', and so lack perspective as to how various pieces of legislation accumulate into a whole. Lord Sumption contended, quite bluntly, that, for 'single-issue pressure groups, public law is politics by other means'[12].

For these groups, one of the virtues of judicial activism is that it allows them to by-pass the messy business of winning the electorate's support. In effect, judicial activism and its influence by pressure groups dispossesses the electorate of much of its influence over political decision-making.

Outsourcing authority – depoliticising public life

The success of insulated democracy relies on administrators of state bodies being able to convert political questions into technical or managerial ones. This objective is usually achieved through what the German social theorist Jurgen Habermas has characterised as the 'scientization of politics', referring to the transference of responsibility for decision-making on many key issues to scientists, professionals and administrators[13]. In this way, many political questions are no longer resolved through argument and debate by parliamentarians, but by the pronouncements of scientists and administrators.

The authorities' response to the COVID-19 pandemic offers a striking illustration of how responsibility for the management of this crisis has been transferred from politicians to scientists and experts. Throughout the lockdown in the UK, government officials insisted that they were following the science. After a while, even some scientists became frustrated with the 'following the science mantra' on the grounds that politicians used it to avoid taking responsibility for taking vital decisions[14].

Far from resisting the tendency for professional administrators and experts to colonise areas of decision-making that were hitherto their prerogative, politicians are often keen to outsource this responsibility to experts. Official announcements regarding a particular policy are followed by the assertion that 'we are following the science', or 'research shows...' or 'our policy is evidence-based'. Politicians rarely use the language of right or wrong to justify their decisions, instead hiding behind their experts. In effect, the outsourcing of policy-making to experts signals the idea that the issues they deal with are not political, and certainly not matters for public debate.

The most important consequence of the scientisation of politics is that it effectively depoliticises public life and truncates the space within which decisions can be questioned. Unlike a policy based on political choice, the 'evidence' cannot be a subject of debate, and the role assigned to citizens is to listen and not question the wisdom of the experts. Important areas of decision-making are thus transformed into no-go areas for democratic accountability.

In the United States, the trend towards converting political issues into technical matters was fervently welcomed by its supporters as meaning 'the end of ideology'. This trend was enthusiastically celebrated by the political scientist Robert E. Lane, who in 1966 argued that in the new 'knowledgeable society', democracy had advanced to a stage where conflicting political interests were displaced by the authority possessed by scientific knowledge[15].

The depoliticisation of public life has also been promoted through outsourcing responsibility for decision-making to supranational administrative agencies. In the post-war years, many national governments have willingly ceded responsibility for policy-making in areas such as finance, trade and the environment to international institutions. Such technocratic institutions have gained significant influence, especially through the medium of the evolving institutions of the European Union, which have successfully assumed responsibility for decision-making over a growing range of issues that used to be the prerogatives of national legislatures. This process of decision-making expressly liberates itself from the burden of accountability and violates traditional norms of the constitutional separation of powers. In this way, it is as if policies appear from nowhere. Claude Juncker, the former president of the European Commission, described how this form of technocratic policy-making works. 'We decree something, then float it and wait for some time to see what happens. If no clamour occurs...because most people do not grasp what had been decided, we continue – step by step, until the point of no return is reached'[16].

The significance of insulating decision-makers from the responsibility of democratic accountability became clear during the Eurozone crisis of 2011. The ease with which the economist and banker Lucas Papademos was appointed prime minister of Greece and the non-elected banker Mario Monti as the head of Italy's government is testimony to the effectiveness of the EU's administrative fiat. At the time, European Commission president José Manuel Barroso explained the necessity of technocratic, insulated decision-making in the following terms: the non-democratically appointed governments of Italy and Greece have been installed 'not just because they're technocrats, but because it [is] easier to ask independent personalities to construct political consensus'. Barroso did not need to spell out the main virtue of these 'personalities' was that they were independent of their electorates. For him, effective policy-making meant minimising the distractions thrown up by the process of public accountability.

In addition to depoliticising decision-making through the use of the courts, the supporters of the federalist project in Europe rely on expert and technocratic authority to assume responsibility for policy-making. International relations professor Andrew

Moravcsik outlined the argument for this procedure in the following terms:

> The apparently "counter-majoritarian" tendency of the EU political institutions insulated from direct democratic contestation arises out of factors that themselves have normative integrity, notably efforts to compensate for the ignorance and nonparticipation of citizens[17].

From this standpoint the 'ignorance of citizens' justifies the EU and other counter-majoritarian institutions. Rather than being seen as a problem, the nonparticipation of citizens is perceived by anti-democratic thinkers as essential for the smooth running of an elite-dominated democracy.

Democracy kills democracy – the revival of Plato's thesis

Until the late 1960s, the elitist form of insulated democracy was remarkably successful in managing the aspirations of public opinion. In the aftermath of the upheavals of the 1960s and the onset of the 1970s economic crisis, Western political elites appeared to lose confidence in their ability to maintain the status quo. Their insecurity was often focused on the unpredictability of public opinion and democracy, which was frequently depicted as a source of unreasonable expectations on government. Whereas in the interwar era the threat to democracy itself was principally attributed to the ambition of totalitarian movements, in the 1970s the villain was perceived to be the unrealistic expectations of the public.

The narrative of 'rising expectations' that developed during this period obliquely referred to citizens' aspirations for a greater share of society's economic and political resources. In a coded manner, the problem of rising expectations served as a veiled way of referring to the expanding scale of popular pressure on governments. This obscured a more fundamental problem, which was the Establishment's failure to win the argument about what was reasonable for citizens to expect.

The implications of this narrative for governmentality were spelled out in great detail in a report by the Trilateral Commission, a global network of leading Western political leaders, policy-makers, prominent opinion formers and business executives, which captured the Spirit of the Age. Titled *The Crisis of Democracy; Report on the Governability of Democracies to the Trilateral Commission*, the report offered a depressing account of the challenges facing liberal-democratic societies, revealing a preoccupation with the apparent loss of legitimacy of the institutional arrangements that successfully managed capitalist economies during the post-war economic boom.

The authors of *The Crisis of Democracy* claimed that 'in doubt today are not just the economic and military policies but also the political institutions inherited from the past'; and that throughout the world, observers predict a 'bleak future for democratic government'. Such predictions projected 'the disintegration of civil order, the breakdown of social discipline, the debility of leaders, and the alienation of citizens'. Even the most stable and successful democracies were said to be prey to the forces of disintegration and 'so observers speak of the Vietnamization of America and the Italianization of Britain'[18].

Despite being published during the Cold War, the Trilateral Report was far less worried about the Soviet Union than about the capacity of governments for managing the pressure emanating from their own citizens. *The Crisis of Democracy* openly acknowledged its lack of confidence about the ability of the political elites to make democracy work. This apprehension was based on an intuitive grasp of a historically significant development – the depletion of the cultural and moral capital of the political elites. However, rather than probing the implications of this development, the authors evasively pointed the finger of blame on democracy itself. 'There is deeper reason for pessimism if the threats to democracy arise ineluctably from the inherent workings of the democratic process itself,' the report warned, before asserting that this political system was indeed responsible for encouraging unrealistic expectations by the public.

The report claimed that 'in recent years, the operations of the democratic process do indeed appear to have generated a breakdown of traditional means of social control, a delegitimation of political and other forms of authority, and an overload of demands on government, exceeding its capacity to respond'[19]. In particular, the so-called 'democratic surge' of the 1960s was held responsible for the declining authority of institutions and conventions of social control.

The anti-democratic ethos of this report was most systematically expounded by the American political scientist and policy adviser Samuel Huntington. In his chapter on the situation in the United States, Huntington claimed that the widening of popular participation in the 1960s had led to the 1970s crisis of governability. The effect of what he characterised as the 'democratic surge' was to substantially increase 'governmental activity', which in turn led to a 'substantial decrease in governmental authority'. Huntington contends that the democratic imperative is continually to expand the state's activity, at the expense of authority[20]. Consequently, the 'democratic surge of the 1960s' challenged and weakened all forms of authority in public and private life:

> Authority based on hierarchy, expertise, and wealth all, obviously ran counter to the democratic and egalitarian temper of the times and during the 1960s, all three came under heavy attack[21].

Huntington posed the question of how to deal with what he characterised as 'democratic distemper' – and his only solution was to attempt to downsize the status of democracy. Thus, he suggested that 'democracy is only one way of constituting authority', and it was 'not necessarily a universally applicable one': indeed, 'in many situations the claims of expertise, seniority, experience, and special talents may override the claims of democracy as a way of constituting authority'. However, his main focus was the project of limiting public pressure. For Huntington, apathy was a political virtue since it diminished pressure on the political elites and allowed democracy to work better: 'the effective operation of a democratic political system usually requires some measure of apathy and non-involvement on the part of some individuals and groups'[22].

For Huntington and his fellow authors, the solution to the crisis of authority was the institutionalisation of a form of insulated democracy that substantially reduced popular pressure on the institutions of the state. The problem they identified was the 'overload' of demands on the state[23]. This concept of overload expressed elite anxieties about the ability to manage the aspirations of the democratic electorate. Overload was portrayed as a curse that democracy inflicted on society in general, and on a capitalist economy in particular.

This narrative made its first appearance in Britain in 1975, with the publication of the 'Economic Contradictions of Democracy' by Samuel Brittan and Anthony King's 'Overload: Problems of Governing in the 1970s'. The Italian political scientist Giovanni Sartori echoed this argument in his essay 'Will Democracy Kill Democracy?'[24] Referring back to the authority of Plato, Sartori warned that 'the idea that the government of our fantastically complex, interconnected and fragile societies could be entrusted to millions of discrete wills' was to allow the 'abyss of incompetence' to prevail[25]. From this perspective, the best way of preventing democracy from killing itself was to deactivate the *demos*.

The acclamation of apathy

The ideal condition for the flourishing of insulated democracy is when public life is depoliticised to the point that apathy prevails. Advocates of the virtue of political apathy argue that, 'if the uninformed masses participate in large numbers, democratic self-restraint will break down and peaceful competition among the elites, the central element in the elitist theory, will become impossible'[26]. This sentiment was explicitly endorsed by Huntington, when he warned that an 'excess of democracy' was a problem for society. He believed that 'the effective operation of a democratic political system usually requires some measure of apathy and non-involvement on the part of some individuals and groups'[27].

To a significant extent, the different policies promoting the depoliticisation of public life have succeeded in significantly reducing democratic 'overload'. Despite periodic social upheavals, the last 3 decades of the twentieth century coincided with the rises of apathy, at least in the form of participation in the democratic process. In numerous US presidential elections since 1960, voter participation has steadily declined, from 62.5 per cent of the electorate in 1960 to 50.1 per cent in 1988. In 1996, only 49 per cent of the voting-age population bothered to cast their ballots – the lowest turnout since 1924. The alienation of the public from the political process was particularly striking in relation to the election of 2000, in which only about 50 per cent of registered voters participated. Unlike the election of 1996, where the outcome was seen to be a foregone conclusion, the contest in 2000 was the most open for decades.

According to a Committee for the Study of the American Electorate in 2000, the cumulative effect of voter disengagement during the previous 30 years was that '25 million Americans who used to vote no longer do so'. Yet voter participation in presidential elections appears positively high compared to the ballots cast for candidates running for a seat in the House of

Representatives, where participation has averaged around 35 per cent. The patterns of voter participation began to shift in the first decade of this century. In 2008, 58.2 per cent of the American voting-age population voted in the presidential election. However, a Knight Foundation study carried out in 2019 found that half of Americans don't vote!

More significantly, on both sides of the Atlantic a growing proportion of the electorate decided to abandon traditional party loyalty and voted either for new parties, or for candidates who were anti-political establishment. It is at this point in time that populist movements gained momentum and provoked the anti-populist backlash that prevails to this day. An integral feature of this backlash was an explosion of a new breed of anti-democratic theories. In *Against Democracy*, Jason Brennan preached the virtues of apathy. 'Most citizens are not doing us any favour by voting,' he stated, before noting that 'asking everyone to vote is like asking everyone to litter'[28].

Today, Democracy Panic is expressed through invoking the ghost of Nazism and casting populists into the role of would-be Brownshirts. In this way, a visceral reaction against democracy can be portrayed as its defence. The anti-populist rhetoric of the twenty-first century is different to its nineteenth-century predecessor in one important respect. Anti-mass theories self-consciously directed their animosity at what they regarded as the morally inferior masses. Today's anti-populist rhetoric is far more subtle. It attacks populists for presuming to voice the views of the people, and at the same time, it vehemently insists that the very idea of 'the people' is an outrageous populist fantasy. The insistence that there is no such thing as the people is a central theme promoted by anti-populist commentators. Anti-populists are deadly serious in their attempt to render the people invisible. Grayling asserts that 'the phrase "the people" should be proscribed in the discourse of democracy', since it is a 'demagogue's term'[29]. Taking the *demos* out of democracy by making the people disappear is a principal aspiration of the present day anti-democratic imagination.

Chapter 10

Reinserting the demos into democracy

What are the prospects of democracy in the future? As I write this conclusion in the midst of the Covid-19 crisis, a report published by an American think-tank warns that the pandemic is 'disrupting democracy' worldwide, at a time when 'democracy was already under threat in many places'[1]. Another survey published in *Foreign Affairs* predicts that 'the pandemic is likely to reinforce the democratic recession that has been evident for the past 15 years'[2].

I have little sympathy with these gloomy predictions about a 'democratic recession', since their concern is with the loss of authority of the system of insulated liberal democracies that were established in the second half of the twentieth century. Their concern is for the future of the form of governance that allowed the Western political establishment to effectively avoid democratic accountability. The current anxieties expressed about the crisis of democracy are underpinned by the fear that popular aspirations have become difficult to manage. According to an analyst associated with Hoover Institution, 'today's crisis of democracy reflects too much democracy'![3]

History indicates that whenever the rhetoric of 'too much democracy' gains currency, it is only a matter of time before the moral standing of democracy itself is again put into question. What is certain is that at the present time the very existence of the 'people' is challenged by anti-populist polemicists. They claim that if not an artificial invention, then the invocation of the people is an exercise in exclusion[4]. The invective that anti-democrats hurl at the term 'people' exposes not simply the emotion of hate but also of fear. Democracy Panic is triggered by a vision that perceives the people as a beast not yet tamed.

The animosity directed towards populism has important implications for the culture of democracy. If indeed the people are either a fiction or irredeemably xenophobic and irrational than the very status of the sovereignty of the people and of popular consent as the foundation of government is called into question. Political authority that is based on the claim of representing the people loses its legitimacy if indeed the *demos* does not exist or does not deserve representation. Democracy becomes emptied of meaning when the people are deemed unworthy of representation.

As the previous chapters indicate, democracy can never be taken for granted. Throughout most of history, the political classes had little sympathy for people attempting to find their voice. As we noted, democracy as an ideal barely survived the ravages of centuries of political hostility. Even in those circumstances where societies acclaimed its virtues, democracy served as an ideal that was very rarely allowed to flourish. Though there were genuine attempts to construct a system of representation through which popular consent could be brought into close alignment with the direction of travel of executive power, the realisation of the ideal of democracy has always faced formidable obstacles.

One key reason why the rhetorical affirmation of democracy was so rarely matched by a genuine commitment is because it is almost always perceived and treated instrumentally. This instrumental approach was most famously expressed in Winston Churchill's statement to the effect that, 'democracy is the worst form of government, except for all the others'. Churchill's negative endorsement of democracy communicates a passive sense of resignation that fails to see any inherent virtues in this form of government.

Churchill's pragmatic view of democracy as a means to an end captures the prevailing consensus on this issue. This sentiment is widely articulated by many supporters of liberal democracy, for whom the liberal principle of the rule of law serves as a first-order principle, and democracy as a second-order one. This sentiment is forcefully expressed by Grayling, who claims that 'democracy is not just elections, and can sometimes even exist *de facto* without them', but it cannot exist without the rule of law'[5]. The model of a democracy that exists without elections is one that assigns citizens to the role of a stage army, which can periodically be mobilised to acclaim the decisions arrived at by their superiors.

Contrary to the anti-democratic prejudice that perceives the mass of society as a mob that threatens freedom, most of the time it is the citizens who constitute the most reliable defence against the attempt to encroach on hard-won liberties. Liberty, and the rule of law, are inextricably linked to democracy. Almost all the freedoms that matter to people were achieved through democratic aspirations and struggles. Freedoms were not granted by liberal oligarchs wedded to the idea of the rule of law but were wrested from the powerful through centuries of democratic struggle. Instead of counterposing freedom to democracy, both should be understood as the outcome of the same aspiration.

Democracy is not just a medium for realising the best results. If it is merely seen as a technocratic tool or a 'lesser evil', its potential for endowing public life with meaning and dynamism will go unrealised. Unfortunately, for many decades, democracy was relegated to the role of a medium of governance – and not surprisingly, many people became switched off from politics or adopted an anti-political cynical posture. In such circumstances, voting was often perceived as a pointless ritual, where how one voted did not matter.

Yet democracy is more than a set of procedures. It is an exercise in decision-making, where citizens find ways to have their voices heard and where they can also hear the voices of others. Through its exercise, it fosters a climate that allows public life to flourish. In the public sphere, the individual voter interacts with others as a citizen. It is at this point that politics can bring out the active side of people so that through argument, debate, conflict and acts of solidarity, citizens are not simply 'voters' but active participants in public affairs.

Democracy is a good in and of itself because it provides an opportunity for the potential creative powers of the people to be harnessed to the full. There are no guarantees that people will make sound decisions, and voters are not always right. However, it is through involvement in electing representatives or voting on issues that matter to them that a society is able to understand, assess and in many cases benefit from the insights of its citizens. By acting democratically and being involved – albeit indirectly – in the making of decisions, people can develop their ideas. In some instances, local democratic decision-making and interaction helps forge genuine bonds of solidarity.

In a society of millions of people, the ideal of democracy cannot be fully realised, and the bonds between citizens' involvement can be weakened by geographical fragmentation and scale. However, the very attempt to live democratically is a good in and of itself. A democratic life assists cultural and intellectual development, by stimulating questioning and debate. Living democratically means just that: a life where deliberating and questioning becomes the norm to the point that people's active side comes into its own, and their capacity for making sound choices is enhanced.

Through living democratically, people's sense of independence and inner strength gains strength. As Lasch explained, 'democracy works best when men and women do things for themselves, with the help of their friends and neighbors, instead of depending on the state'[6]. Doing things for yourself should not be interpreted as narrow individualism: rather, such acts signal a determination to take control of life and take responsibility for it. It is through a willingness to assume responsibility for one's actions that solidarity is forged and genuine self-governing communities can be established. Hence encouraging people to find their voice and engage with one another is the precondition for the flourishing of democratic life.

In the end, how we view democracy depends on how we regard human beings and their potential for development, for exercising self-rule and taking responsibility for their community and fellow human beings. Throughout history, anti-democratic theories have directed their animosity towards the majority of people inhabiting their society. In their eyes, these people were their social, economic and moral inferiors. Anti-democratic theories justify the rule of the few on the grounds that most human beings lack the moral and intellectual resources necessary to trust them with determining or influencing the future direction of their society.

Over the centuries, the explicit vilification of the masses has given way to a more indirect and covert narrative. In the twenty-first century, the anti-democratic devaluation of people takes its most strident and coherent form through the discourse used to describe the persona and behaviour of political opponents. Anti-populism, which is the form assumed currently by the historical anti-majoritarian impulse, continually describes its opponents as xenophobic, ignorant and mentally deficient. From this standpoint, people who vote the 'wrong way' are not simply erroneous – they are diagnosed as suffering from a psychological deficit.

A commitment to popular democracy is not inspired by a dogmatic and uncritical worship of people. Citizenship does not confirm automatic virtue on individuals. As Spinoza realised centuries ago, people can arrive at very bad decisions and unleash powers of destruction. There are numerous examples of public displays of hysterical and irrational behaviour. However, the response to the dilemma faced by Spinoza is not to give in to the temptation of turning one's back on democracy, but to provide greater scope for its expression. Usually, blaming the people serves as a way of avoiding responsibility for developing ideas and arguments that can help others to gain a measure of confidence and clarity. Taking responsibility for the development of an enlightened public life is not an act of paternalistic charity, but the first step towards protecting the freedom of all. Instead of the language of blame, we need to ask the question of why we have not managed to develop arguments that can persuade our fellow citizens to embrace a more positive course of action.

The spirit of democracy encourages all of us to take each other seriously. That is why we argue and debate with one another and need the freedom to express ourselves in accordance with our views and inclinations. Free speech is the foundation of all the other freedoms required for the flourishing of democracy. Individuals cannot play the role of citizens until they find their voice.

The more that people feel that their voice counts, the more likely it is that public life will come alive and enhance the quality of our political imagination. That for millions of people, politics has become a dirty word is an indictment of a governmental culture that prefers to de-politicise issues rather than open them up to public debate. The negative anti-political trends that signal the idea that somehow politics is to blame for many of our problems constitutes a negation of democracy. There is nothing positive or radical about anti-politics – it simply expresses the conviction that the pursuit of democratic decision-making is futile.

The flipside of the rejection of politics is the acceptance of the world as it is. In contrast, democratic politics assumes that the choices people make can make a difference. It constitutes a refusal to defer to Fate. Constant references to the crisis of democracy should not be allowed to obscure the fact that it still remains an ideal that motivates millions of people. The instinct that has driven so many people to refuse to defer to Fate has ensured that the spirit of democracy could survive all the many attempts to undermine its appeal.

Numerous forms of governments have come and gone – theocracies, oligarchies, absolute monarchies, totalitarian dictatorships – but more than 2500 years on from its birth, the idea of democracy alone continues to endure and inspire. Why? Because as long as people aspire to be free, the vision of politically equal citizens governing themselves inspires the human imagination like no other political ideal. The war against democracy will continue into the indefinite future but the vision that shapes its core values will survive all attempts to defeat it.

It is pertinent to the current context to note that, historically, Democracy Panic was most strikingly expressed through its description of democracy as a deathly virus. In 1841, drawing attention to this supposed perilous disease, the Reverend Joshua Brooks explained that 'we have seen France, Belgium, Italy, Poland, and other places, affected by the revolutionary spirit, the chief incitement to which is the *democratic virus*'[7]. Thankfully, democracy has proved infectious. But, unlike Covid-19, the infectious quality of democracy has brought out the best qualities of the human spirit.

Giving voice to the people

Today, in a hesitant way, people are trying to find their voice. What unites the different movements labelled as populists is their rejection of elite culture and the values it promotes. Despite the attempt to represent populist movements as a distinct political species, they have little in common other than their opposition to ideals and the political practices of technocratic governance. Throughout the world, many people feel estranged from their governments and institutions. They feel patronised by advocates of technocratic governments and have become sceptical towards the so-called truths communicated by professional politicians and experts.

Of course, people speak with different voices, are motivated by diverse concerns and are drawn towards a variety of heterogeneous solutions. Many of the reactions and attitudes associated with populism constitute what Hannah Arendt would have characterised as the search for pre-political bonds and solidarity. The common quest for gaining meaning through the forging of pre-political solidarity can often express itself in different political forms. That is why populist aspirations can lead people to embrace a variety of contradictory political standpoints – sentiments such as the search for social justice and equality to anti-immigrant chauvinism can attach themselves to the quest for solidarity.

In the long run, the authority of the competing cultural and political influences will determine the outcome of the current wave of anti-technocratic populist movement. In the short term, through its challenge to the values and the language of the system of technocratic governance, populist sentiments help foster a climate where public life can be re-politicised and democratised. Populist sentiments can play an important role in reviving a culture of political participation and democratic debate. However, the mere rejection of the values of the elites on its own does not constitute a positive and viable alternative to the politics of technocratic governance.

What is needed is not simply the rejection of the prevailing anti-*demos* culture, but a positive political alternative that promotes the values of democracy and social solidarity. The crystallisation of the populist impulse into a political movement that infuses the aspiration for solidarity with the ideals of popular sovereignty, consent and an uncompromising commitment to liberty would be a cause well worth fighting for.

Practising democracy involves a willingness to experiment. That is why US Supreme Court Justice Louis Brandeis referred to local communities as 'laboratories of democracy'. As is the case with all experiments, that of democracy does not come with guarantees. But it provides citizens with an opportunity to test

Endnotes

Foreword

1   A video of this discussion is available on https://www.youtube. com/watch?v=JtFF11qBQGI

2   https://www.theguardian.com/politics/2019/jul/14/alastair-campbell-on-the-populist-virus-and-why-bill-shorten-lost

3   John Keane 'The Pathologies of Populism', 29 September 2017, *The Conversation,* https://theconversation.com/the-pathologies-of-populism-82593

4   https://www.japantimes.co.jp/opinion/2020/03/31/commentary/world-commentary/virus-kill-populism-make-stronger/#. Xqf1A9NKglI

5   https://www.wsj.com/articles/will-coronavirus-kill-populism-11585004780

6   https://www.theatlantic.com/magazine/archive/2019/12/too-much-democracy-is-bad-for-democracy/600766/

7   https://www.economist.com/democracy-in-america/2009/12/17/when-too-much-democracy-threatens-freedom

8   Londonderry (1849) p. 261.

9   This argument is made by the historian Simon Schama. See https://www.telegraph.co.uk/news/2016/11/10/simon-schama-defends-comparing-donald-trumps-election-win-to-th/

10 For example see https://theprint.in/world/plato-was-right-democracy-always-creates-tyrannical-leaders/323059/

Chapter 1

1   Clare Foges, 'We need Big Brother to beat this virus', *The Times*: 20 April, 2020.

2   See https://asiatimes.com/2020/04/covid-19-is-an-affront-to-democracy/

3   See https://www.law.cornell.edu/supremecourt/text/285/262

4   See Furedi (2007)

5   Grayling (2017) p11.

6   See Lee (2012), Maclean, N. (2017) *Democracy in Chains*, & Runciman, D. (2018)

7   https://www.theatlantic.com/magazine/archive/2016/07/how-american-politics-went-insane/485570/

8   Lasch (1995) pp. 3 and 24.

9   See Furedi (2013).

10   Fukuyama (1992) p. 45.

11   Kaltwasser (2014) p. 470.

12   Brennan (2016) p. ix.

13   Zakaria (1997) p. 25.

Chapter 2

1   Ober (1998) p. 35.

2   See the discussion in Thornton (2000) p. 120.

3   See Donlan (1973) for a discussion of the tradition of anti-aristocratic thought in Greek poetry.

4   See discussion in Ober (2017), p. 29.

5   Thornton (2000) p. 223.

6   See Dahl (1989) p. 14.

7   Vlastos (1952) p. 103.

8   Ober (1998), p. 35.

9   Cited in http://hrlibrary.umn.edu/education/thucydides.html

10   Ober (1998) p. 35.

11   Ober (2017) p. 22.

12   McClelland (1988) pp. 1-2.

13   See Furedi (2013) Chapter 3 for a discussion of these cultural trends.

14   Goody & Watt (1963) p. 321.

15   Goody & Watt (1963) p. 332.

16   Goody & Watt (1963) p. 333.

17   Euben (1997) p. 65.

18   Thornton (2000) p. 170.

19   See https://www.pewresearch.org/fact-tank/2015/11/20/40-of-mill

ennials-ok-with-limiting-speech-offensive-to-minorities/

20   Ober (1998) p. 190.

21   Plato (1997), Phaedrus, p. 275.

22   Cited in Pope (1988) p. 282.

23   Protagoras 319b-d, See http://classics.mit.edu/Plato/protagoras.
      html

24   See *Crito* (47b10-11) http://classics.mit.edu/Plato/crito.html

25   https://nymag.com/intelligencer/2016/04/america-tyranny-donald-
      trump.html

26   https://qz.com/1293998/2400-years-ago-plato-saw-democracy-
      would-give-rise-to-a-tyrannical-leader-filled-with-false-and-
      braggart-words/

Chapter 3

1   Arendt (1960) p. 67.

2   See Nyirkos (2018) p. 40.

3   See Saxonhouse (1996) p. 2.

4   Hume (2017) p. 111.

5   Cited in Hume (2017) p. 111.

6   Stone (1986) p. 96.

7   Wilson (2009) p. 216.

8   Sharpe (2000) p. 31

9   Stone (1986) p. 96.

10   Milton (1999) p. 23.

11   Hobbes Cited in Lloyd (2002) p. 39.

12   See Oakeshott (2006) p. 293.

13   Wood (1991) p. 56.

14   Machiavelli (2009) p. 116

15   https://avalon.law.yale.edu/18th_century/fed09.asp

16   Cited in http://brownpoliticalreview.org/2016/07/tyranny-in-brit
      ain/

17   See http://press-pubs.uchicago.edu/founders/documents/v1ch16
      s15.html

18   See https://avalon.law.yale.edu/18th_century/fed10.asp

19   http://brownpoliticalreview.org/2016/07/tyranny-in-britain/

20   Tuck (2016) p. 7.

21   Saxonhouse (1996) p. 15.

22   Saxonhouse (1996) p. 12.

23   Bendix (1978) p. 321.

24   Cited by Anton Jäger 'The Myth of Populism', *Jacobin Magazine*, https://jacobinmag.com/2018/01/populism-douglas-hofstadter-donald-trump-democracy

25   See the interesting reflections of the historian Vann Woodward (1938) p. 207.

26   Willoughby (1917) p. 635.

27   Grayling (2017) p. 127.

Chapter 4

1   Feuer (1987) p. 139.

2   Spinoza (2007) p. 18.

3   Spinoza (2007) p. 181.

4   Feuer (1987) p. ix.

5   Feuer (1987) p. 64.

6   Cited in Feuer (1987) p. 80.

7   Cited in Feuer (1987) pp. 87-88.

8   Diderot is cited in Krieger (1975) p. 53.

9   Israel (2006).

10   The argument contained in this essay is developed at length in Furedi (2013).

11   See http://www.columbia.edu/acis/ets/CCREAD/etscc/kant.html

12   See Kant (2007) p. 37.

13   Cited in Cavanaugh (1969) p. 57.

14   Cited in Marini (1967) p. 463.

15   Cited in Palmer (1969) p. 128.

16   Israel (2010) p. 1.

17   Laski (1936) pp. 213-214.

18   Kant is cited in Bobbio (2005) p. 17.

19   Fromm (1965) p. 3.

20 Cited in Fromm (1965) p. 3.

Chapter 5

1 Prochaska (1972).
2 Cites James Mill (anonymously) 'The Ballot', *Westminster Review*, vol. xiii (1830) p. 2.
3 Mill (1820) pp. 31-32.
4 See Wilson (1955) p. 488.
5 Jaeger, H (2010) p. 3.
6 Sheehan (2002) p. 937.
7 He noted that, 'Popular clamour may be said to be that sort of feeling, arising from the passion of a multitude acting without consideration; or an excitement created amongst the uneducated, or amongst those who do not reflect, or do not exercise their judgement on the point in question.' MacKinnon (1971) p. 18.
8 MacKinnon (1971) p. 17.
9 Lewis (1974) p. 249.
10 Lewis (1974) p. 251.
11 Mill (1840) p. 45.
12 Mill (1861) p. 383.
13 Mill (1861) p. 378.
14 Saint-Simon is cited in Wolin (2004) p. 338.
15 Hamilton (2008) p. 49.
16 Hamilton (2008) p. 49.
17 Ten (1969) p. 67.
18 Cited in Burns (1968) p. 315.
19 Tocqueville (1998) p. 103.
20 Tocqueville (1998) p. 104.
21 Cited in Shepard (1909) p. 42.
22 P.H. Colomb 'The Patriotic Editor in War', *National Review*, April 1987, p. 253.
23 E.A. Ross (1896) p. 767.
24 Wilson (1955) p. 506.
25 https://www.theatlantic.com/magazine/archive/2016/07/how-

american-politics-went-insane/485570/

Chapter 6

1   Cited in Marcuse (2008) p. 74.

2   Wallas (1961) p. 243..

3   http://pinkmonkey.com/dl/library1/revolt.pdf , p. 7.

4   See Marcuse (2013).

5   Adorno (1950) p. 420.

6   Adorno (1950) p. 418.

7   Cited in https://www.rollingstone.com/politics/politics-features/why-were-living-in-the-age-of-fear-190818/

8   Laski (1919) p. 28.

9   Dewey (1931) p. 26.

10 Ginsberg (1964) pp. 141-142.

11 Ginsberg (1964) p. 134.

12 Lasswell (1927) p. 148.

13 Palmer (1967) p. 252.

14 Mannheim (1943) pp. 14–15.

15 Cited in Giner (1976) p. 141.

16 Mannheim (1940) p. 63.

17 Legutko (2016) pp. 29 & 59.

18 Adorno (1950) pp. 418 & 420.

Chapter 7

1   Soffer, (1969) p. 111.

2   See Richards (2002) p. 161.

3   See Le Bon (1897).

4   See Nye (1975).

5   Nye (1975) p. 13.

6   Childs 919350 p. xi.

7   Doob and Robinson (1935) p. 89.

8   Doob and Robinson (1935) p. 94.

9   Lasswell (1965) p. 19.

10 Lasswell (1965) p. 19.

11   Lasswell (1965) pp. 19-20.

12   Cited in Frezza (2007) p. 139.

13   Cited in Nuttall (2005) p. 674.

14   Cited in Nuttall (2005) p. 674.

15   Adorno (1950) p. 429.

16   Lasch (2013) p. 44.

17   See https://harpers.org/archive/1964/11/the-paranoid-style-in-ame rican-politics/

18   See Robin (2001).

19   Lipset (1964) p. 114.

20   Eysenck (1960) p. 137.

21   Nai & Martinez (2019) p. 1367.

22   Singh (1998) p. 13.

23   Lasch (2013) p. 153.

24   Walker (1966) p. 287.

25   Morris-Jones (1954) p. 25.

26   Cited in Justman (1998) p. 78.

27   Quassim Cassam, 'Why extremism is a question of psychology, not politics', *New Statesman*, 18 February 2018.

28   Krastev (2007) p. 74.

29   https://time.com/4381837/brexit-psychology/

30   See https://thepsychologist.bps.org.uk/volume-32/december-2019/ we-must-turn-tide-brexit-psychodrama

31   See https://www.vox.com/2016/6/25/12029786/brexit-uk-eu-immi gration-xenophobia

32   See https://blogs.scientificamerican.com/mind-guest-blog/trump-s-victory-and-the-neuroscience-of-rage/

33   See https://www.spectator.co.uk/article/can-we-trust-the-people-i-m-no-longer-sure

34   Brennan (2016).

35   Bagehot (1872) p. 117.

36   Matthew Campbell 'Italian election: Roman elite tremble over "ignorant beasts" at the gate', *The Times*, 27 May 2018, https:// www.thetimes.co.uk/article/roman-elite-tremble-over-ignorant-

beasts-at-the-gate-f2j3j6j07

Chapter 8

1   Bosanquet, Bryant, and Ross (1908-09) p. 64.

2   Soffer (1969) p. 132.

3   Ball (1987) pp. 47-48.

4   Ball, T. (1987) 'Authority and Conceptual Change' in Pennock, J.R. abd Chapman, J.W. (1987) (eds.) *Authority Revisited*, New York University Press: New York, p. 48.

5   Ball, (1987) p. 51.

6   Matthew Flinders and Gergana Dimova 'Bringing in the experts: blame defection in the COVID-19 crisis', *LSE British Politics And Policy Blog*, 3 April 2020, https://blogs.lse.ac.uk/politicsandpolicy/bringing-in-the-experts-blame-deflection-and-the-covid-19-crisis/

7   Tocqueville.

8   See Lenzer (1998) p. lii.

9   Cited in Ten (1969) p. 315.

10   Cited in Burns (1968) p. 315.

11   See King (1999).

12   Dicey (1920) p. lxxvii.

13   King (1999) p. 15.

14   The conservative critic Michael Tanner is cited in King (1999) p. 16.

15   Shepard (1935) p. 6.

16   Shepard (1935) p. 18-19.

17   Frezza (2007) p. 145.

18   See Frezza (2007) p. 147.

19   Bernays (1947) p. 113.

20   Bernays (1947) p. 115.

21   Bernays (1947) p. 115.

22   Pimbert & Wakeford (2001) p. 23.

23   Smith & Wales (2000) p. 55.

24   Smith & Wales (2000) p. 52.

25   See Thompson & Hoggett (2000) p. 352 and Hoggett and Thompson (2002) p. 120.

26   See The discussion in Furedi (2018) pp. 164-166.

27   Matt Motta 'Had enough of experts?', 30 August, 2017. https://blogs.lse.ac.uk/usappblog/2017/08/30/had-enough-of-experts-anti-intellectualism-is-linked-to-voters-support-for-movements-that-are-skeptical-of-expertise/

28   Norris and Inglehart (2019) p. 5.

29   https://amp.theguardian.com/world/2020/apr/23/scientists-criticise-uk-government-over-following-the-science

Chapter 9

1   Loewenstein, K. (1937a) p. 418.

2   Loewenstein (1937a) p. 428.

3   Loewenstein (1937b) p. 652.

4   Loewenstein (1937b) p. 657.

5   See Maddox (2019).

6   Council of Europe, 'Compass: manual for Human Rights; education with Young people', https://www.coe.int/en/web/compass/democracy

7   Heartfield (2013) p. 72.

8   Muller (2012) p. 40.

9   Muller (2013) p. 128.

10   Lind (2020) pp. 62-62.

11   https://whorunsbritain.blogs.lincoln.ac.uk/2013/12/14/sense-and-sensibility-politicians-judges-and-the-rise-of-judicial-review/

12   Habermas (1987) p. 63.

13   See https://www.dailymail.co.uk/news/article-8258845/Politicians-hiding-follow-science-mantra-warns-scientist.html

14   See Lane (1966).

15   Cited in Lind (2020) p. 54.

16   Cited in Heartfield (2012) p. 56.

17   Crozier, Huntington & Watanuki (1975) p. 2.

18   Crozier, Huntington & Watanuki (1975) p. 8.

19   Huntington (1975) pp. 64 and 103.

20   Huntington (1975) p. 75.

21   Huntington (1975) pp. 113 and 114.

22   Crozier, Huntington and Watanuki (1975) p. 8.

23   See Parsons (1982) for a discussion of these texts.

24   Sartori (1975) p. 158.

25   Walker (1966) p. 287.

26   Huntington (1975) pp. 37-38.

27   https://www.politico.com/news/magazine/2020/02/19/knight-nonvoter-study-decoding-2020-election-wild-card-115796

28   Brennan, (2016) p. xi.

29   Grayling (2017) p. 170.

Chapter 10

1   https://carnegieendowment.org/2020/04/06/how-will-coronavirus-reshape-democracy-and-governance-globally-pub-81470

2   Richard Haas 'Not Every Crisis is a Turning Point', *Foreign Affairs*; 7 April, 2020.

3   See https://www.hoover.org/research/democratic-distemper.

4   Kelly (2017) p. 521.

5   Grayling (2017) p. 32.

6   Lasch (1995).

7   Brooks (1841) p. 298.

Bibliography

Adorno, T.W. 'Democratic Leadership and Mass Manipulation' in Gouldner, A. (1950) ed. *Studies in Leadership; Leadership and Democratic Action*, Harper & Brothers: New York.

Arendt, H. (1960) 'What is Freedom?' in Arendt, H. (2006) *Between Past and Future*, Penguin: London.

Bagehot, W. (1872), *Physics and Politics*, Henry S. King & Co.: London.

Ball, T. (1987) 'Authority and Conceptual Change' in Pennock, J.R. and Chapman, J.W. (1987) (eds.) *Authority Revisited*, New York University Press: New York.

Bendix, R. (1978) *Kings or People; Power and the Mandate to Rule*, University of California Press: Berkeley.

Bernays, E.L. (1947) 'The engineering of consent', *The Annals of the American Academy of Political and Social Science*, 250(1).

Bobbio, N. (2005) *Liberalism and Democracy*, Verso Books: London.

Bosanquet, B., Bryant, S. & Ross, G.R.T. (1908-09) 'The Place of Experts in Democracy. A Symposium', *proceedings of the Aristotelian Society, New Series*, vol. 9.

Brennan, J. (2016) *Against Democracy* (2016) PUP : Princeton, NJ.

Brooks, J.W. (1841) 'Elements of Prophetical Interpretation', *The Literalist*, vol. 2, part 1.

Burns, J.H. (1968) 'J.S. Mill and democracy' in Schneewind, J.B. (1968) *Mill; A Collection of Critical Essays*, Macmillan: London.

Canovan, M. (1996) *Nationhood and Political Theory*, Edward Elgar: Cheltenham.

Cavanaugh, J.G. (1969) 'Turgot: The rejection of enlightened despotism', *French Historical Studies*, vol. 6, no. 1.

Childs, H. L. (1935) 'Introduction to pressure groups and propaganda', *Annals of the American Academy of Political and Social Science*, vol. 179.

Dahl, R.A. (1989) *Democracy and Its Critics*, Yale University Press:

New Haven.

Dewey, J. (1931) *Individualism: Old and New*, George Allen & Unwin Ltd: London.

Dicey, A.V. (1920) *Lectures on the Relation Between Law & Public Opinion in England During the Nineteenth Century*. Macmillan and Company: London.

Doob, L.W. and Robinson, E.S. (1935) 'Psychology and propaganda', *Annals of the American Academy of Political and Social Science*, vol. 179.

Donlan, W., (1973) 'The tradition of anti-aristocratic thought in early Greek poetry', *Historia: Zeitschrift für Alte Geschichte*.

Eysenck, H.J. (1960) *The Psychology of Politics*. Praeger: New York.

Feuer, L.S. (1987) (originally 1958) *Spinoza and the Rise of Liberalism*, Transaction Books: New Brunswick, NJ.

Frezza, D. (2007) *The Leader and the Crowd: Democracy in American Public Discourse, 1880–1941*, University of Georgia Press: Athens, GA.

Fromm, E. (1965) (originally published 1941) *Escape from Freedom*, Henry Holt and Company: New York.

Fukuyama, F. (1992) *The End of History: and The Last Man*, Simon and Schuster: New York.

Furedi, F. (2007) 'The changing meaning of disaster'. *Area*, vol. 39, no. 4.

Furedi, F. (2013) *Authority: A Sociological History*, Cambridge University Press: Cambridge.

Furedi, F. (2018) *How Fear Works: The Culture of Fear in the Twenty-First Century*, Bloomsbury Press: London.

Giner, S. (1976) *Mass Society*, Martin Robertson & Company Limited: London.

Ginsberg, M. (1964) (originally 1921) *The Psychology of Society*, Methuen: London.

Goody, J. and Watt, I. (1963), 'The consequences of literacy', *Comparative Studies in Society and History*, vol. 5, no. 30.

Grayling, A.C. (2017) *Democracy and its Crisis*, Oneworld

Publications.

Habermas, J. (1987) *Toward a Rational Society*, Polity Press: London.

Hamilton, A. (2008) 'J.S. Mill's Elitism. A Classical Liberal's Response to the Rise of Democracy', in Kofmel, E. (2008) (ed) *Anti-Democratic Thought*, Imprint-Academic: Exeter.

Heartfield, J. (2013) *The European Union and The End Of Politics*, Zero Books: Winchester UK.

Hofstadter, R. (1964) *The paranoid style in American politics*, Vintage: New York.

Hume, M. (2017) *Revolting! How The Establishment Are Undermining Democracy And What They're Afraid Of*, William Collins: London.

Huntington, S. (1975) 'The United States', in Crozier, M., Huntington, S. and Watanuki, J. (1975) *The Crisis of Democracy; Report on the Governability of Democracies to the Trilateral Commission*, New York University Press: New York.

Huntington, S. and Watanuki, J. (1975) *The Crisis of Democracy; Report on the Governability of Democracies to the Trilateral Commission*, New York University Press: New York.

Israel, J. (2006) *Enlightenment Contested: Philosophy, Modernity, and the Emancipation of Man, 1670–1752*, Oxford University Press: Oxford.

Israel, J. (2010) *A Revolution of the Mind: Radical Enlightenment and the Intellectual Origins of Modern Democracy*, Princeton University Press: Princeton NJ.

Israel, I. (2011) *Democratic Enlightenment: Philosophy, Revolution, and Human Rights, 1750-1790*, Oxford University Press: Oxford.

Jaeger, H. (2010) 'Before "world opinion": "public opinion" and political community before the twentieth century', Paper presented at the SGIR 7th Pan-European International Relations Conference, Stockholm, 9–11 September, 2010.

Justman, S. (1998) *The psychological mystique*, Northwestern University Press: Evanston, Illinois.

Kaltwasser, C.R. (2014) 'The Responses of Populism to Dahl's Democratic Dilemmas', *Political Studies*, vol. 62, no. 3.

Kant, I. (2007) *Perpetual Peace*, FQ Classics: Oxford.

Kelly, D. (2017) 'Populism and the History of Popular Sovereignty'. In *The Oxford Handbook of Populism*, Oxford University Press: Oxford.

Kendra, J. and Wachtendorf, T. (2002) 'Elements of Resilience in the World Trade Center Attack', preliminary report published by the Disaster Research Center, DRC, University of Delaware: Newark, DE.

King, D., 1999. *In the name of liberalism: illiberal social policy in the USA and Britain*. Oxford University Press: Oxford.

Krastev, I. (2007) 'The strange death of the liberal consensus', *Journal of Democracy*, vol. 8, no. 4.

Krieger, L. (1975) *An Essay on the Theory of Enlightened Despotism*, The University of Chicago Press: Chicago, IL.

Lane, R.E. (1966) 'The decline of politics and ideology in a knowledgeable society' *American Sociological Review*, vol. 31, no. 5.

Lasch, C. (1985.) *The Minimal Self: Psychic survival in troubled times*, WW Norton & Company: New York.

Lasch, C. (1995) *The Revolt of the Elites: and the Betrayal of Democracy*, W.W. Norton & Company, New York.

Lasch, C. (2013) *The True and Only Heaven: Progress and Its Critics*, Norton: New York.

Laski, H. (1919) *Authority in The Modern State*, Yale University Press: Yale.

Laski, J.H. (1936) *The Rise Of European Liberalism*, George Allen & Unwin: London.

Lasswell, H. (1927) *Propaganda Techniques in the World War*, Knopf: New York.

Lasswell, H. (1965) (originally published in 1935) *World Politics and Personal Insecurity*, The Free Press: New York.

Le Bon, G., 1897. *The crowd: A study of the popular mind*. T. Fisher

Unwin: London.

Lee R.H. (2012) *Saving Democracy from Suicide,* CreateSpace Independent Publishing Platform.

Legutko, R. (2016) *The Demon in Democracy: Totalitarian Temptations in Free Societies,* Encounter Books: New York.

Lenzer,G.(1998) *Auguste Comte and Positivism,* Transaction Books: Piscataway, N.J

Levitsky, S. and Ziblatt, D., 2018. *How democracies die.* Viking Books: New York.

Lewis, G. C. (1974) (originally published 1849) *An Essay on the Influence of Authority in Matters of Opinion,* Arno Press: New York.

Lind, M. (2020) *The New Class War: Saving Democracy from the Metropolitan Elite,* Atlantic Books: London.

Lippmann, W. (1922) *Public Opinion,* Macmillan: New York.

Lipset, S.M. (1964). *Political man: The social bases of politics,* Mercury Books: London.

Londonderry, R.S. (1849) *Memoirs and Correspondence of Viscount Castlereagh, Second Marquess of Londonderry, vol. 4,* Henry Colburn: London.

Loewenstein, K., (1937a), 'Militant democracy and fundamental rights, I', *American Political Science Review,* vol. 31, no. 3

Loewenstein, K., (1937b) 'Militant democracy and fundamental rights, II, '*American Political Science Review,* vol. 3i, no. 4.

Lloyd, S.A. (2002) *Ideals as Interests in Hobbes's Leviathan; the Power of Mind over Matter,* Cambridge University Press: Cambridge.

Machiavelli, N., 2009. *Discourses on Livy.* University of Chicago Press: Chicago.

MacKinnon, W.A, (1971) (1828) *On the Rise, Progress and Present State of Public Opinion in Great Britain and Other Parts of the World,* Irish University Press: Shannon, Ireland.

Maclean, N. (2017) *Democracy in Chains,* Viking Press, New York.

Maddox, G. (2019, 'Karl Loewenstein, Max Lerner, and militant democracy: an appeal to "strong democracy"'. *Australian*

Journal of Political Science, 54(4).

McClelland, J. S. (1988) *The Crowd and the Mob: From Plato to Canetti*. Unwin: London.

McKeown, R. (1951) (ed) *Democracy in a World of Tensions: A Symposium Prepared by UNESCO*, Chicago University Press: Chicago.

Mannheim, K. (1940) *Man and Society in an Age of Reconstruction*, Routledge: London.

Mannheim, K. (1943) *Diagnosis of Our Time: Wartime Essays of a Sociologist*, Routledge & Kegan Paul Ltd: London.

Marcuse, H. (2008) (originally published 1936) *A Study on Authority*, Verso: London.

Marcuse, H., 2013. *One-dimensional man: Studies in the ideology of advanced industrial society*. Routledge: London.

Marini, F. (1967) 'Popular sovereignty but representative government: the other Rousseau', *Midwest Journal of Political Science*, vol. 11, no. 4.

Mill, J. (1820) 'Government' in *Essays on Government, Liberty of the Press, and Law of Nations*, London: J. Innes,1825, A.M. Kelley [reprint edition] 1967: New York.

Mill, J. S. (1840) 'Democracy in America', *Edinburgh Review*, vol. 63.

Mill, J. S. (1861) 'Considerations on Representative Government', in Mill, J. S. (2008) *On Liberty and Other Essays*, Oxford University Press: Oxford.

Milton, J. (1999), *Areopagitica and other Political Writings of John Milton*, Indianapolis, IN: Liberty Fund.

Morris-Jones, W. H. (1954) 'In Defense of Apathy', *Political Studies*, vol. 2.

Müller, J.W. (2012) 'Beyond Militant Democracy', *New Left Review*, 73.

Müller, J.W. (2013) *Contesting Democracy: Political Ideas in Twentieth Century Europe*, Yale University Press: New Haven.

Nai, A. & Martinez Coma, F, (2019) 'The personality of populists:

provocateurs, charismatic leaders, or drunken dinner guests?', *West European Politics*, vol. 42, no. 7.

Norris, P. & Inglehart, R. (2019) *Cultural backlash: Trump, Brexit, and authoritarian populism.* Cambridge University Press: Cambridge.

Nuttall, J. (2005), 'Labour Revisionism and Qualities of Mind and Character, 1931–79', *The English Historical Review*, 120.

Nye, R. (1975) *The Origins of Crowd Psychology and the Crisis of Mass Democracy in the Third Republic*, Sage: London.

Nyirkos, T. (2018) *Tyranny of The Majority: History, Concepts, And Challenges*, Routledge: London.

Oakeshott, M. (2006) *Lectures in the History of Political Thought*, Imprint Academic: Exeter.

Ober, J. (1989) *Mass and Elite in Democratic Athens; Rhetoric, Ideology, And The Power*, Princeton University Press: Princeton.

Ober, J. (1998) *Political Dissent in Democratic Athens; Intellectual Critics of Popular Rule*, Princeton University Press.

Ober, J. (2017) *Demopolis: Democracy Before Liberalism in Theory and Practice*, Cambridge University Press: Cambridge.

Palmer, R. R. (1969) *The Age of the Democratic Revolution: The Challenge*, Princeton University Press: Princeton.

Parsons, W. (1982) 'Politics Without Promises: The Crisis of "Overload" and Governability', *Parliamentary Affairs*, vol. 35, no. 4

Pimbert, M and Wakeford, T. (2001) 'Overview – Deliberative Democracy and Citizen Empowerment', *PLA Notes*, 40.

Plato (1997), Phaedrus, in J. M. Cooper (ed.) (1997), *Plato: Complete Works*, Indianapolis, IN: Hackett,

Plato(1997a), Republic, in J. M. Cooper (ed.) (1997), *Plato: Complete Works*, Indianapolis, IN: Hackett.

Pope, M. (1988) 'Thucydides and Democracy', *Zeitschrift fur Alte Geschichte*, vol. 37, no. 3

Prochaska, F.K. (1972) 'Thomas Paine's The Age of Reason Revisited', *Journal of the History of Ideas*, 33(4).

Richards, G. (2002) *Putting Psychology in Its Place: A Critical Historical Overview*, Routledge: London

Robin, R. (2001) *The Making of the Cold War Enemy; Culture and Politics in the Military-Intellectual Complex*, Princeton University Press: Princeton.

Ross, E. A. (1896) 'Social control II. Law and public opinion', *The American Journal of Sociology*, vol. 1, no. 6

Runciman, D. (2018) *How Democracy Ends*, Profile: London.

Sartori, G. (1975) 'Will democracy kill democracy? Decision-making by majorities and by committees', *Government and Opposition*, 10(2).

Saxonhouse, A.W. (1996) *Athenian democracy: Modern Mythmakers and Ancient Theorists*, University of Notre Dame Press: Notre Dame, Indiana.

Sharpe, K. (2000), *Reading Revolutions: The Politics of Reading in Early Modern England*, Yale University Press: New Haven, CT

Sheehan, C. (2002) 'Madison and the French Enlightenment: The Authority of Public Opinion', *William and Mary Quarterly*, vol. 59, no. 4

Shepard, W. J. (1909) 'Public opinion', *The American Journal of Sociology*, vol. 15, no. 1.

Shepard, W.J., 1935. 'Democracy in transition', *American Political Science Review*, vol. 29, no. 1.

Singh, N.P. (1998) 'Culture/wars: recoding empire in an age of democracy', *American Quarterly*, vol. 50, no. 3.

Smith, G. & Wales, C. (2000) 'Citizens' Juries and Deliberative Democracy', *Political Studies*, vol. 48.

Soffer, R.N. (1969) 'New Elitism: Social Psychology in Prewar England', *Journal of British Studies*, vol. 8, no. 2.

Spinoza, B. (2007) *Theological-Political Treatise*. Ed. Jonathan Israel. Trans. Michael Silverthorne and Jonathan Israel. Cambridge: Cambridge University Press.

Stanley, J. (2018) *How Fascism Works: The Politics of Us and Them*, Random House: New York.

Ten, C. L. (1969) 'Mill and Liberty', *Journal of the History of Ideas*, vol. 30, no. 1.

Thompson, S, & Hoggett, P. (2000) 'The Emotional Dynamics of Deliberative Democracy', *Policy & Politics*, vol. 29, no. 3.

Thornton, B. (2000) *Greek Ways: How the Greeks Created Western Civilization*, Encounter Books: San Francisco.

Tocqueville, de A. (1998) *Democracy in America*, Wordsworth Editions: London.

Tuck, R. (2016) *The Sleeping Sovereign: The Invention of Modern Democracy?* Cambridge University Press: Cambridge.

Van Woodward, C. (1938) *Agrarian Rebel: Biography of Tom Watson*, The Beehive Press: Savannah Georgia.

Vlastos, G. (1952) 'Presocratic Theology and Philosophy', *Philosophical Quarterly*, 2.

Wallas, G. (1961) (originally published in 1908) *Human Nature In Politics*, Constable : London.

Walker, J.L. (1966) 'A critique of the elitist theory of democracy', *American Political Science Review*, vol. 60. no. 2.

Whitehead, A.F. (1979) *Process and Reality*, Free Press: Glencoe, Ill.

Willoughby, W. W. (1917) 'The Prussian theory of monarchy', *The American Political Science Review*, vol. 11, no. 4.

Wilson, B. (2009) *What Price Liberty?* Faber and Faber: London

Wilson, F. G. (1955) 'Public opinion and the middle class', *The Review of Politics,* vol. 17, no. 4

Wolin, S. (2004) *Politics and Vision*, Princeton University Press: Princeton, NJ.

Wood, N. (1991) 'Some reflections on Sorel and Machiavelli', *Political Science Quarterly'* vol. 83, no. 1, p. 56.

Zakaria, F., 1997. 'The rise of illiberal democracy', *Foreign Affairs*, 76.

CULTURE, SOCIETY & POLITICS

The modern world is at an impasse. Disasters scroll across our smartphone screens and we're invited to like, follow or upvote, but critical thinking is harder and harder to find. Rather than connecting us in common struggle and debate, the internet has sped up and deepened a long-standing process of alienation and atomization. Zer0 Books wants to work against this trend. With critical theory as our jumping off point, we aim to publish books that make our readers uncomfortable. We want to move beyond received opinions.

Zer0 Books is on the left and wants to reinvent the left. We are sick of the injustice, the suffering and the stupidity that defines both our political and cultural world, and we aim to find a new foundation for a new struggle.

If this book has helped you to clarify an idea, solve a problem or extend your knowledge, you may want to check out our online content as well. Look for Zer0 Books: Advancing Conversations in the iTunes directory and for our Zer0 Books YouTube channel.

Popular videos include:

Žižek and the Double Blackmain

The Intellectual Dark Web is a Bad Sign

Can there be an Anti-SJW Left?

Answering Jordan Peterson on Marxism

Follow us on Facebook
at https://www.facebook.com/ZeroBooks and Twitter at https://
twitter.com/Zer0Books

Bestsellers from Zer0 Books include:

Give Them An Argument
Logic for the Left
Ben Burgis
Many serious leftists have learned to distrust talk of logic. This is
a serious mistake.
Paperback: 978-1-78904-210-8 ebook: 978-1-78904-211-5

Poor but Sexy
Culture Clashes in Europe East and West
Agata Pyzik
How the East stayed East and the West stayed West.
Paperback: 978-1-78099-394-2 ebook: 978-1-78099-395-9

An Anthropology of Nothing in Particular
Martin Demant Frederiksen
A journey into the social lives of meaninglessness.
Paperback: 978-1-78535-699-5 ebook: 978-1-78535-700-8

In the Dust of This Planet
Horror of Philosophy vol. 1
Eugene Thacker
In the first of a series of three books on the Horror of Philosophy,
In the Dust of This Planet offers the genre of horror as a way of
thinking about the unthinkable.
Paperback: 978-1-84694-676-9 ebook: 978-1-78099-010-1

The End of Oulipo?
An Attempt to Exhaust a Movement
Lauren Elkin, Veronica Esposito
Paperback: 978-1-78099-655-4 ebook: 978-1-78099-656-1

Capitalist Realism
Is There No Alternative?
Mark Fisher
An analysis of the ways in which capitalism has presented itself
as the only realistic political-economic system.
Paperback: 978-1-84694-317-1 ebook: 978-1-78099-734-6

Rebel Rebel
Chris O'Leary
David Bowie: every single song. Everything you want to know,
everything you didn't know.
Paperback: 978-1-78099-244-0 ebook: 978-1-78099-713-1

Kill All Normies
Angela Nagle
Online culture wars from 4chan and Tumblr to Trump.
Paperback: 978-1- 78535-543-1 ebook: 978-1-78535-544-8

Cartographies of the Absolute
Alberto Toscano, Jeff Kinkle
An aesthetics of the economy for the twenty-first century.
Paperback: 978-1-78099-275-4 ebook: 978-1-78279-973-3

Malign Velocities
Accelerationism and Capitalism
Benjamin Noys
Long listed for the Bread and Roses Prize 2015, *Malign Velocities*
argues against the need for speed, tracking acceleration
as the symptom of the ongoing crises of capitalism.
Paperback: 978-1-78279-300-7 ebook: 978-1-78279-299-4

Meat Market
Female Flesh under Capitalism
Laurie Penny
A feminist dissection of women's bodies as the fleshy fulcrum of
capitalist cannibalism, whereby women are both consumers and
consumed.
Paperback: 978-1-84694-521-2 ebook: 978-1-84694-782-7

Babbling Corpse
Vaporwave and the Commodification of Ghosts
Grafton Tanner
Paperback: 978-1-78279-759-3 ebook: 978-1-78279-760-9

New Work New Culture
Work we want and a culture that strengthens us
Frithjoff Bergmann
A serious alternative for mankind and the planet.
Paperback: 978-1-78904-064-7 ebook: 978-1-78904-065-4

Romeo and Juliet in Palestine
Teaching Under Occupation
Tom Sperlinger
Life in the West Bank, the nature of pedagogy and the role of a university under occupation.
Paperback: 978-1-78279-637-4 ebook: 978-1-78279-636-7

Ghosts of My Life
Writings on Depression, Hauntology and Lost Futures
Mark Fisher
Paperback: 978-1-78099-226-6 ebook: 978-1-78279-624-4

Sweetening the Pill
or How We Got Hooked on Hormonal Birth Control
Holly Grigg-Spall
Has contraception liberated or oppressed women?
Sweetening the Pill breaks the silence on the dark side of hormonal contraception.
Paperback: 978-1-78099-607-3 ebook: 978-1-78099-608-0

Why Are We The Good Guys?
Reclaiming Your Mind from the Delusions of Propaganda
David Cromwell
A provocative challenge to the standard ideology that Western power is a benevolent force in the world.
Paperback: 978-1-78099-365-2 ebook: 978-1-78099-366-9

The Writing on the Wall
On the Decomposition of Capitalism and its Critics
Anselm Jappe, Alastair Hemmens
A new approach to the meaning of social emancipation.
Paperback: 978-1-78535-581-3 ebook: 978-1-78535-582-0

Enjoying It
Candy Crush and Capitalism
Alfie Bown
A study of enjoyment and of the enjoyment of studying. Bown asks what enjoyment says about us and what we say about enjoyment, and why.
Paperback: 978-1-78535-155-6 ebook: 978-1-78535-156-3

Color, Facture, Art and Design
Iona Singh
This materialist definition of fine-art develops guidelines for architecture, design, cultural-studies and ultimately social change.
Paperback: 978-1-78099-629-5 ebook: 978-1-78099-630-1

Neglected or Misunderstood
The Radical Feminism of Shulamith Firestone
Victoria Margree
An interrogation of issues surrounding gender, biology, sexuality, work and technology, and the ways in which our imaginations continue to be in thrall to ideologies of maternity and the nuclear family.
Paperback: 978-1-78535-539-4 ebook: 978-1-78535-540-0

How to Dismantle the NHS in 10 Easy Steps (Second Edition)
Youssef El-Gingihy
The story of how your NHS was sold off and why you will have to buy private health insurance soon. A new expanded second edition with chapters on junior doctors' strikes and government blueprints for US-style healthcare.
Paperback: 978-1-78904-178-1 ebook: 978-1-78904-179-8

Digesting Recipes
The Art of Culinary Notation
Susannah Worth
A recipe is an instruction, the imperative tone of the expert, but this constraint can offer its own kind of potential. A recipe need not be a domestic trap but might instead offer escape – something to fantasise about or aspire to.
Paperback: 978-1-78279-860-6 ebook: 978-1-78279-859-0

Most titles are published in paperback and as an ebook. Paperbacks are available in traditional bookshops. Both print and ebook formats are available online.
Follow us on Facebook
at https://www.facebook.com/ZeroBooks
and Twitter at https://twitter.com/Zer0Books